Psychologist Rob Yeung, PhD, is a researcher, coach and keynote speaker in the areas of human communication, influence and persuasion, change and high achievement. He is the author of over a dozen international bestsellers, including *Confidence: The Power to Take Control and Live the Life You Want* and *I is for Influence: The New Science of Persuasion.* As well as teaching at universities and business schools, he is an in-demand expert on television, providing specialist comment on CNN and BBC News as well as programmes such as *Big Brother.* He has written for the *Financial Times*, the *Daily Telegraph* and the *Guardian* and has been quoted in publications ranging from *Men's Health* and *Glamour* to the *Wall Street Journal.*

www.robyeung.com

www.twitter.com/robyeung

Other books by Rob Yeung

YOU CAN CHANGE YOUR LIFE

Easy Steps to Getting What You Want

ROB YEUNG

MACMILLAN

First published 2012 by Macmillan
an imprint of Pan Macmillan, a division of Macmillan Publishers Limited
Pan Macmillan, 20 New Wharf Road, London N1 9RR
Basingstoke and Oxford
Associated companies throughout the world
www.panmacmillan.com

ISBN 978-0-230-76382-1

5 7 9 8 6 4

A CIP catalogue record for this book is available from
the British Library.

Designed and set by seagulls.net
Printed and bound by CPI Group (UK) Ltd, Croydon, CR0 4YY

Visit **www.panmacmillan.com** to read more about all our books
and to buy them. You will also find features, author interviews and
news of any author events, and you can sign up for e-newsletters
so that you're always first to hear about our new releases.

CONTENTS

INTRODUCTION

'Things do not change; we change.'
Henry David Thoreau

Every year, millions of people try to change their lives. Many want to lose weight or get fitter. Some would like to improve their relationships with loved ones, quit bad habits or start healthy ones. Others are keen to change jobs, learn new skills or improve their financial situations. More than a few wish they could socialise more, become more self-confident or be happier. And the good news is: *you can change your life.*

A good friend of mine, whom I'll call Michael, keeps telling me how he wishes he could change his life. A man in his early forties, he runs a small business, a computer consultancy. Actually, he *is* the business – both boss and sole employee. He travels the country running courses for people who need to get to grips with a specialist piece of financial software.

Sadly, he hates his job. He runs through the exact same training session day after day, answering more or less the same questions month after month. He's away from home at least a couple of nights a week and ends up checking into one featureless, grey hotel after the next. He says it's like being in a time warp or a really dull, financial accounting version of the movie *Groundhog Day.*

Michael hasn't been in a relationship for years either. He's a lean man with thick dark hair, a square jaw and a generous smile who looks like he should be a sports coach or personal trainer. He could be a real catch for the right woman, but after a long week at work, the last thing he wants to do is to trawl bars and nightclubs. Neither does he feel obliged to try online dating.

'It's just not me,' he maintains.

For now, his dreams sustain him. In his fantasies, Michael sees himself running a thriving consultancy with perhaps a dozen people working for him internationally. He would sit at the head of this buzzing company, watching both plaudits and profits roll in. And then he might have the time to meet the right woman and live happily ever after.

'Daydreaming about some distant horizon may actually make our goals *less* likely to come true'

It was an evening several winters ago when he first mentioned his dream to me. Fuelled by more than a handful of late-night whiskies in a swanky bar, he spelt out how he wished his life could be.

Nothing's changed yet. But it's good to have a dream, right? It makes sense that having a positive picture of the future should keep us focused on our goals and inspired to achieve them.

Actually, no.

The thing is: daydreaming about some distant horizon may actually make our goals *less* likely to come true. And we know it's true because there's *proof*.

Imagine for a moment that you've been asked by research psychologists to describe your daydreams, your wishes and fantasies about the future. The researchers ask you to write down what you hope for. Once you've recorded your thoughts, they thank you and that ends the experiment. Or so you think.

Two years later, the psychologists come back to see how you're getting on in life. They ask you how your career is going, what you're up to, and how much you're earning.

That's exactly what psychologists at the University of Hamburg did. They asked a group of final-year university students about the positive thoughts, images or fantasies they had about leaving university and making a successful transition into the world of work.

Not all of the undergraduates had positive fantasies. But those who did were asked to describe their career-related dreams and fantasies by writing them down. Some dreamed about having lavish offices and good-looking colleagues working for them. Others contemplated big salaries and the possessions they could buy with their newfound wealth. They were also asked to rate how frequently they experienced such thoughts and images on a 10-point scale (where 1 = 'very rarely' to 10 = 'very often').

Fast-forward two years to when the psychologists sent out a follow-up survey to find out how the (now) graduates were doing in their careers. Had they progressed in line with their dreams? Startlingly, individuals who had frequently dreamed about a bright future while still at university were earning *less* money than those who reported fewer positive fantasies. The daydreamers also reported having sent out fewer job applications and been offered fewer jobs – proof perhaps that they had put less effort into their job-hunting than those who were more grounded in reality.'[1]*

In other words, the more frequently a student had experienced positive fantasies about their future careers, the *less* successful they became. Rather than serving to inspire and galvanise them into action, their fantasies and wishes for good things had sapped their energy. It made them less likely to take charge, less likely to succeed.

> 'If you want to understand the real principles that help people to achieve change, you're in the right place'

The implications for my friend Michael aren't terribly good then. The research tells us that the more he fixates on the best-case scenario of what he might achieve, the less likely he is to achieve it.

Unfortunately, Michael isn't alone.

Many books recommend that readers bring to mind vivid pictures of the lives that they want to achieve. The authors of such books say that painting a clear image of the future will help us to realise it. Regrettably, research tells us that those authors are wrong.

If you want to understand the real principles that help people to change their lives – and discover the myths that are often perpetuated about change – you're in the right place.

---

* You'll find numbered notes throughout the book. Most readers can enjoy the book without turning to the notes at all. Notes are provided principally for the more academically minded readers who may wish to read the original scientific papers, perhaps to further their own research.

THE SCIENCE OF CHANGE
AND PERSONAL IMPROVEMENT

As a psychologist, my job is to help people change their lives. Some have specific goals: they want a new job or want to feel more confident when socialising and dating, for example. Others have broader goals, such as wanting to understand why they're not content – they often wish to overhaul their lives and become happier.

When I counsel people on changing their circumstances, I aim to suggest only tools and techniques that work – ones that are backed by scientific evidence. After all, if you went to see a doctor at a hospital about a pain in your chest, you'd want to know that his advice was based on research, on proven strategies and treatments that would get rid of the pain as effectively as possible. You wouldn't go to a self-taught quack who simply has some personal experience of having got rid of his own chest pain or, worse yet, a charlatan who advocates chanting and wishful thinking in the belief it might help.

'I aim to suggest only tools and techniques that work – ones that are backed by scientific evidence'

As a consequence, I'm very wary of most so-called self-help books. Many self-help 'gurus' are well intentioned but misguided. They too often base their recommendations on their own experience, on their personal theories about what will or won't help people to change. But without quantifiable evidence that their techniques work, their advice might be ineffective or even woefully harmful.

Fortunately, researchers all over the world – from medical specialists and psychologists to neuroscientists and economists – are constantly conducting studies on what does help folks to change. They're finding out what might inadvertently block us from making change successfully too.

In such studies, researchers go to tremendous pains to prove what works and what doesn't. Long before they can begin actually testing their techniques on people, they must submit detailed applications about their intentions to university ethics boards for discussion and approval. Next, they must persuade dozens, hundreds or in some cases perhaps thousands of volunteers to agree to being tested. After weeks, months or even years of observing their volunteers, the researchers then have to write up their methods and results for scrutiny by other investigators. Only then are they allowed to publish their findings. And it's only through such diligent, rigorous studies that we know what tactics genuinely help or unfortunately hinder us in changing and improving ourselves.

I know because those are the exact same hoops I learnt to jump through at the start of my career. When I was considering how to conduct my own experiments, I had to think carefully about whether my methods would stand up to intense scrutiny by my fellow researchers. Once I had collected my data, I had to send my results out to experts in the field who wanted to understand exactly how I had come to my conclusions. Only then was I allowed to publish my results in scientific journals.

Such investigations sometimes throw up surprising findings that may go against what we otherwise believe. For example, the

University of Hamburg study we encountered earlier demonstrates rather elegantly that spending too much time transporting ourselves to overly positive visions of the future isn't a good idea should we want to alter our lives. Contrary to what many self-help gurus recommend, it appears that the more we dream, the *less* likely we may be to achieve our goals. ·

Hundreds of similar investigations are carried out every year on the psychology of change and personal improvement. And, having surveyed this vast body of research, my aim with this book is to present a comprehensive analysis of lasting change – about what can both help us to change *and* hamper us from achieving it. I want to debunk common myths and misconceptions about change and recommend only approaches that have been proven to work.

Yes, including the scientific evidence means that this book is possibly a more challenging and less straightforward read than some other self-improvement books. However, I am confident that you would rather be informed about *why* to do things as opposed to being told only *what* to do.

EMBARKING ON THE QUEST FOR CHANGE

As a psychologist, my professional interest in helping people began with the three years of research I undertook for my PhD. I'll come to that in a minute, but my *personal* interest in change started a few years before. Between the first and second years of my undergraduate degree – I'd just turned 19 at the time – I spent six weeks of my summer in Fremont, California, with my cousin Peter and his family. When I arrived in the sun-drenched state, a new gym had opened up nearby which was handing out three-month free trial memberships. So we signed up.

I'd never used a gym before so I was unsure of how to use the machines. I didn't know whether to push or pull or turn and twist. But I persevered.

I didn't notice much difference in my fitness level from one day to the next. But when I returned to university in the UK, I began to get compliments from friends. I'd never been sporty when I was growing up. But after that Californian summer, friends noticed that my body had changed shape – my chest and shoulders had got broader. Girls wanted to touch my new biceps; they pulled my T-shirt up and marvelled at my abs.

But this was more than just a physical transformation; I felt transformed on a deeper level too. I had a newfound sense of belief in myself and my ability to take on new challenges. It was a life-changing moment; I felt more confident interacting with people – friends, tutors, strangers at parties. Even my grades went up. I'd been a strictly average student in my first year at university – I'd had to retake an exam that I'd failed the first time around – but I shot up to become one of the top 5 per cent by the end of my second year.

It was as if making a change in one area of my life boosted my confidence to take on larger changes in other areas. Positive change became self-rewarding.

Of course, my experience – or indeed any single person's experience – doesn't necessarily mean the same positive effects for everyone. But we'll see in a later chapter there's hard evidence showing that exercise really *does* benefit us all psychologically as well as physically.

After I'd finished my undergraduate degree, I decided that I wanted to continue my studies with a doctorate in psychology. Getting fitter had made such a difference to me that I wanted to spread the word: I chose to spend three years delving into the field of sport and exercise psychology.

When I started exploring the published research in the field, I unearthed a stunning fact. Even though millions of people all over the world make New Year's resolutions to get fit and lose weight every year, around 50 per cent of them give up after only a few months. And it happens every year. Despite their best intentions, so many people fail year after year to change their lives, to achieve something that they wanted.

Neither is the 50 per cent figure restricted solely to exercise. When people attempt to give up smoking, around half of them fall short within six months and find themselves hooked on cigarettes once more. The same goes for people wanting to eat more healthily or drink less alcohol. Despite the desire to change, so many people fail to change their lives.

'Introducing even small tweaks into our lives can create a virtuous cycle of fulfilment and further change'

I decided in my PhD to investigate ways of facilitating change. In particular, I wanted to help people to lose weight through physical exercise.

That was more than a few years ago. But my motivation to help people to make change happen in their lives has stuck with me. Whether people want to shape up physically or mentally, it's my job to help them get to where they want to be.

Change can be so rewarding. Introducing even small tweaks into our lives can create a virtuous cycle, an upward spiral, a self-perpetuating process of fulfilment and further change. Make a small change and we feel somewhat better about ourselves. Feel better and we feel more confident and capable of changing more. After a while, even the bigger changes that at first seemed out of reach may be well within our grasp.

NAVIGATING THROUGH THIS BOOK

Whether you want to change something in your life or want to help the people around you – perhaps partners or loved ones, friends or colleagues – to change theirs, I hope you will find the evidence-based advice in this book not only fascinating but also useful. Make no mistake. I'm not promising overnight transformations or instant miracles. As we've seen, you don't get things in life simply by wishing for them to come true. But in this book you will find the best, most up-to-date thinking on the skills, beliefs and methods that you can use to help make change happen.

'You don't get things in life simply by wishing for them to come true'

As we forge on through each chapter, I'll illustrate the various principles and techniques with stories culled from my own experience – examples of friends and case studies of clients I've worked with. In many cases, I've disguised names and some personal information to preserve people's anonymity, but I hope that these recollections will help you to see how the science can be put into action.

How can we make plans that will give us the best shot of achieving our aspirations? How can the right friends help us to achieve our goals – and why might the wrong friends actually derail our good intentions? Given that change is difficult, how can we handle the occasional lapse or even outright failure? These are the sorts of questions we'll tackle over the course of this book. To help you understand how best to go about making change happen – either in your own life or in the lives of those around you – I've structured the book into seven chapters as follows:

➡ **Chapter One: Getting Ready for Change**
There's a joke amongst psychotherapists which isn't that funny but is actually rather true: 'How many therapists does it take to change a light bulb?' Answer: 'One, but the light bulb has to *really want* to change.' The same is true of people wanting to tweak their own lives. Whether you're trying to change aspects of your life or would like to assist someone else to change theirs, this chapter will get you started on the journey towards improvement by helping you to generate a strong desire for change.

➡ **Chapter Two: Setting Effective Goals**
On 1 January every year, millions of people all over the world make New Year's resolutions to lose weight, switch jobs or otherwise change their lives. Unfortunately, many of them

fail. Thankfully, science has identified the key characteristics of effective goals. In this chapter, I'll share with you the latest findings about setting goals that will give you the very best chance of success.

⇒ Chapter Three: Boosting Our Will to Succeed

Perhaps the biggest impediment to change is ourselves or, to be more precise, our occasional lack of willpower. We're all tempted to do the wrong thing at times. We might feel too tired to go to the gym or too lazy to do that extra bit of studying. When trying to give up smoking or unhealthy foods, we may find ourselves too strongly drawn to a cigarette or on the cusp of saying 'yes' to that chocolate dessert. But the good news is that we can hone our ability to steer clear of temptation and stick with our goals. Science tells us that, just as we can train our muscles at the gym, we can bulk up our willpower too. So in this chapter, we shall discover how to improve our self-discipline and resolve.

⇒ Chapter Four: Seeing Success

Many athletes swear by the power of visualisation in helping them to quell nerves and boost motivation before they step into the sporting arena. Likewise, many self-help gurus claim that picturing the lives we'd like to attain can help us to achieve them. So both athletes and self-help advisors claim that using mental imagery can help us to accomplish our goals. Why is only one of these two groups right and the other one very, very wrong? In this chapter, I'll both shed some light on the apparent confusion and explain how to use visualisation as a powerful technique for making changes in our lives.

➡ **Chapter Five: Developing Greater Emotional Resilience**

Whenever we try to modify what we do – perhaps to do away with bad habits or establish new ones – it's only natural that we may falter occasionally. On the hunt for that perfect new job, we may find ourselves experiencing more than a handful of rejections from interviews. Or if we're trying to overcome shyness, anxiety or depression, we may still experience dark days. How can we keep our spirits up when we feel down and success seems elusive? Psychologists have identified *proven* tactics for bouncing back in the face of adversity and we'll explore a handful of them here.

➡ **Chapter Six: Tapping into People Power**

Concerned parents forever worry about the company that their children keep. But it turns out that it's not only impressionable kids and teenagers who are influenced in their behaviour by the people around them. Indeed, our capacity for change is more affected by other people than we may realise. Of course, it's human nature to gravitate towards supportive friends who urge and encourage us on. But psychological sleuths have found that it's not always what our friends *say* that matters. So what does? In this chapter, I'll answer that question and cover how we can make the best use of the people in our lives – and why we might sometimes need to steer clear of certain others.

➡ **Chapter Seven: Racing Towards the Finish Line**

I've read more than a handful of self-help authors claiming that you can make change happen in only 28 or 21 days – or even as little as 7 days. But that's not how lasting change works. I worry that people who have unrealistic expectations of the change process may feel frustrated and want to give up when they don't get results swiftly enough. So in this chapter, I shall explain what the latest experiments tell us about change and how people can make it happen.

OVER TO YOU

As we move from chapter to chapter, we'll cover dozens of research studies. I'll do my best to explain the implications of each one – what it means, whether you're trying to change yourself or goad someone else to change. But on occasion, the ramifications may be so critically important that I will want to summarise them in a box like this one.

Some of the recommendations thrown up by the research may at first glance seem obvious, but there will be modern twists on them that you may not have encountered. Other recommendations may be surprising or even completely contradict what you've previously heard.

I hope that this book will be both enlightening and entertaining. In discovering how best to tackle change, we'll encounter lots of interesting, sometimes exciting and occasionally counterintuitive findings. We'll look at the results of some truly ingenious, almost mad scientist-inspired experiments involving everything from deception to minor forms of torture. We'll look at the secrets that top athletes and sportspeople use to stay motivated and help them to succeed. We'll discuss why doing something as small as saying 'no' to a slice of cake may help us to boost our resolve when it comes to just about anything else we may want to achieve too. And we'll discuss why you'd be crazy *not* to talk to yourself at least occasionally.

Thousands of people every day manage to change their lives. And when you're ready to kick off your own personal change project (or help others with theirs), I've included a separate collection of resources at the very end of the book, which I've divided into two parts.

The first is called *The Change Manifesto*. It starts on page 237 and is a step-by-step guide for changing things in your own life. In 12 steps, you will put together your own change project based on the latest research.

Then on page 257, we have *The Motivation Toolkit*, which covers the best methods for bolstering your confidence and giving you a shot of motivation whenever you need it. Taking these two parts together, whether you're changing a tiny bad habit or revamping your entire life, you will have all of the best tools and techniques gathered in one place at the end of the book.

You *can* change your life. Are you ready to get started?

ONE
GETTING READY FOR CHANGE

'If you don't like something, change it.
If you can't change it, change your attitude.'
Maya Angelou

A close friend called Joshua is very overweight. He's about average height but so rotund that he grumbles about the narrow seats on both trains and planes. What's more, he complains that several high-street clothes stores don't make trousers wide enough for him. Doctors would categorise him as clinically obese or even what they call morbidly obese.

As a psychologist, I help people to make change in their lives and we often talk about how he can change his life. Regrettably, it's not Joshua's weight that we discuss.

In his late thirties, Joshua wears rimless glasses and has the world-weary look of someone who's seen and done it all. He originally trained as a journalist and began his career as a news reporter, travelling up and down the country to cover the latest political scandals, health scares, corporate misadventures and the like. At the moment, he works in the marketing team for a women's clothing chain. He writes a witty, insightful blog about the modern man's perspective on women's fashion. Think of a male version of Carrie, the central character in the TV series *Sex and the City*, and you won't go far wrong.

Unfortunately, he finds his job soul-destroying. He finds the work superficial and he feels like a sell-out given his journalistic training. So I talk to him about new career options. Even though I would much prefer to help him with his weight – to save his life, perhaps – I can't.

Now, I'd be delighted to help him to lose weight. When I was researching my doctorate in sport and exercise psychology, I also trained as a personal trainer. I continue to work as a psychologist and coach too. So I *know* I could be of assistance. But I feel that it's not my place. He has never asked for help in losing weight, so for me to force my opinions on him would feel like interfering. More importantly, though, research shows that people can't *be* changed. They have to *want* to change.

GIVING PEOPLE A NUDGE IN THE RIGHT DIRECTION

Given that you've picked up a book on change, I'm guessing that you want to change something about yourself, your situation or your life. Perhaps you realise that you're unhappy at work and would rather be running your own business but don't know where to start. Or you have an emotional issue that you want to

'People can't *be* changed. They have to *want* to change'

address – maybe you shy away from social gatherings or you lose your temper and lash out inappropriately.

You may or may not have tried to change in the past – say you signed up to an Internet dating website but never got around to meeting anyone. Or you made a New Year's resolution to be more assertive with people but eventually fell back into your ingrained habits.

You probably have a good idea of *what* you'd like to change. But *why* do you want to change exactly?

Sure, you may be able to think of a couple of good reasons straightaway. But seriously, how much thought have you really given it? Because the science tells us that having your very own reasons matters.

The evidence comes from a carefully conducted experiment, of course. The researchers in charge of the study, led by social psychologist Barbara Müller at Radboud University Nijmegen in the Netherlands, duped several dozen regular smokers into taking part in an experiment allegedly assessing their ability to argue for or against different points of view. I say 'duped' and 'allegedly' because as is fairly standard practice in many psychological experiments, the volunteers were temporarily deceived as to the true aims of the study – at least until they were tested, prodded and observed to the researchers' satisfaction.

Each of the volunteers was ushered into a laboratory individually and, without their knowledge, was randomly allocated to one of two conditions. Participants in the first, experimental condition were asked to spend five minutes writing down as many arguments as they could come up with as to why smoking was undesirable. Participants assigned to the second, control condition were simply asked to read a page of pre-prepared arguments against smoking.

Individuals from both conditions were then told that the next part of the experiment was supposed to involve taking a computerised test. But – uh-oh – there seemed to be trouble with the computer. After a couple of minutes of fiddling with the computer, the experimenter explained to each volunteer that a glitch with the software meant that the test would be delayed while an engineer attempted to sort it out.

Again, another falsehood told by Müller and her team. In reality there was no problem with the software. There wasn't a computerised test to take at all.

'Have a seat and relax,' the experimenters told the volunteers. 'It'll only take fifteen minutes to fix the issue.'

And that was the third and final untruth as the experimenters deliberately left each participant in the study alone for twice as long as they said they would. Why? All of these steps were orchestrated to leave each volunteer alone, feeling bored and frustrated. The researchers then secretly observed the hapless volunteers to see how many of them would find the tension of waiting so unbearable that they would need to light up a cigarette.

Only a third of the control group (37 per cent) who read pre-prepared statements arguing against smoking managed to last the full 30 minutes. However, more than two-thirds of the experimental group (71 per cent) who had generated their own arguments against smoking managed to wait the full 30 minutes without needing to smoke.[2]

The researchers looked at the lists of reasons the experimental group had come up with and found that they were remarkably similar to the lists that had been prepared in advance for the control group to read. So it wasn't that the experimental participants had come up with any particularly original or ingenious arguments against smoking. No, the sole difference seemed to be that the experimental participants had been actively involved in coming up with their own reasons against smoking.

It's such a small yet powerful intervention. Spending just five minutes writing down reasons against smoking somehow persuaded more of the experimental participants that it really wasn't a good idea to smoke.

The implications of the study are plain. When we want to change other people's behaviour, we should steer clear of presenting them with our opinions or the so-called facts. We'd be better off asking them to come up with their own, personal reasons for change.

So if you want to persuade loved ones to do more exercise, for example, don't harangue them about the health benefits. Instead, you might bring up the topic and then ask them to consider it for themselves: 'If you were fitter, what do you think it would allow you to do differently?' Or if you want to convince lonely single friends to get out onto the dating scene, avoid lecturing them about how much they might enjoy meeting new people. Try asking them, 'Do you ever miss having someone special in your life?' and 'What do you miss about being in a relationship?'

'We don't like to feel pushed or pressurised into doing things against our will'

The implications may even be useful for convincing colleagues, customers and members of the general public to modify their behaviour. Suppose you're trying to get people to do more for the planet. Rather than hectoring them about the harm they're doing to the environment, try asking them, 'Why do you think it might be a good idea to recycle?'

If we stop to think about it, the effectiveness of the indirect approach makes sense. After all, think about the times people have told you that you *should* or *must* do something. We hate being nagged. We don't like to feel pushed or pressurised into doing things against our will. And neither, it turns out, do other people.

Tell people why they should behave differently and their defences go up. But ask them *why* they might want to change and you may get a much, much better result.

FINDING OUR OWN MOTIVES FOR CHANGE

When we want to modify our own behaviour, it may pay dividends to identify our specific reasons for wanting to do so too. Many of us have the feeling that our lives could be better if we made some changes. But there's a big difference between feeling dissatisfied (but simply putting up with something) and actually taking the action to make things happen.

Ready to take that first step now?

OVER TO YOU

If you're serious about changing something in your life, take five minutes to list as many good reasons as you can for wanting to change. Take a fresh sheet of paper, a double-page spread in your notebook or open up a document on your computer – you'll need more space than just the margin of this book – and write down the benefits and advantages of making that change in your life. In psychological parlance, these are called 'outcome expectancies' – i.e. the positive outcomes that you could expect to attain if you were to achieve your aims. What would you gain? What might you be able to do differently? In what ways might you feel better?

For example, your initial thought may be that you 'want to be more confident'. But research suggests that it may be more helpful to pinpoint *why* you want to become more confident. Is it to help you in social situations such as making friends and dating? To become more assertive when dealing with pushy colleagues at work? To feel more comfortable telling your partner how you'd like him or her to make more of a contribution to the relationship? Or all of those reasons and more besides?

If you really want to help yourself to stay motivated to change, start making your list of reasons now. Remember that this list is just for you, to boost your motivation, so feel free to scribble everything and anything down, even if you suspect that your friends or family might find some of the reasons superficial or silly.

Next, weigh up the disadvantages of not making the change and just accepting things as they are. What are the downsides? What grievances do you have about your situation? What are the risks or dangers that you might encounter in the future if you were to stay the same?

Let's think about the reasons people may have for changing. For example, the benefits of incorporating more fruit and vegetables into your diet could include losing weight and having more regular bowel movements. The dangers of *not* eating more fruit and vegetables might include an elevated risk of vitamin deficiencies or even bowel cancer.

The benefits of, say, deciding to set up a book club might include making more friends, becoming less lonely as well as reading a broader range of books. The downsides of *not* setting up a book club might include fewer opportunities to engage your mind as well as missing out on the chance to meet brand new friends and possibly even a new boyfriend or girlfriend.

Last year, I coached a client who wanted to quit her job and set up her own small business. At the time, Jacinta was working as the personal assistant to an influential producer in the entertainment industry. A compact forty-something woman with a shock of bright auburn hair and a penchant for extravagant jewellery, she had been doing the job for over 15 years but the nature of the work had changed recently. For a start, her boss, Peter, had moved the business from offices in central London to a suite of rooms at his own home north of London, which added an extra hour to Jacinta's commute to work each way. And then, perhaps because her boss was running the business from his own home, he had become more demanding, more verbally aggressive and downright unpleasant to work for. Despite being only in her mid-forties, she looked as world-weary and beaten down as someone who was nearing the end of her career rather than its midpoint.

When Jacinta came to me, she was conflicted about what to do. While she didn't enjoy the working environment and the lengthy commute, she also recognised that she was well paid and had a regular income. Her business idea: to sell a range of skincare products that her sister had stumbled upon in continental Europe that was as yet unavailable in the UK. However, the thought of starting up this new business was daunting, if not downright scary. There was no guarantee of success either.

I suggested that she list the pros of setting up her business and the cons of staying where she was. We didn't meet up for another coaching session for a month or so, but she emailed me a list of arguments for changing:

Benefits of starting my own business	Downsides of staying where I am
A feeling of control over my own destiny.	Peter's barrage of complaints whenever he thinks I've made a mistake (when it's usually his fault).
Being able to tell people at parties that I'm the managing director of a business.	Commuting three to four hours a day.
Recognition for my efforts rather than just being someone else's assistant.	Feeling emotionally blackmailed that I'm crucial to the company.
The freedom to work when I choose rather than when someone else chooses.	Lack of career progression – what happens when Peter eventually retires?
Not dying of a stress-induced heart attack!	Peter's occasional, supposedly jokey comments about my weight or age.
The knowledge that whatever I earn will be for me and me alone.	Nasty instant coffee at the office.
Working with a product that I personally believe in.	Having to go to Peter's awful annual summer and Christmas parties.

When we met again, Jacinta had made up her mind. She said that typing up her thoughts made the choice more obvious. Working through the arguments for quitting her job made her certain that it was the right thing to do. In fact, she was staggered by how clear-cut the decision seemed. Her only regret was that it had taken so long for her to realise it.

There's a happy ending to the story: she set up her online skincare business and, while it's still small, it's growing. And despite having to work possibly longer hours, she feels more in control and invigorated by the work rather than drained as she had been by her previous job.

We are all likely to have our own highly personal if not downright unconventional lists. The reasons you might wish to become more assertive, study for a qualification, grow your social circle or whatever else will almost certainly differ from the reasons that might spur on even your close friends to do the same.

'The more individualised our lists of reasons for change, the more likely we may be to stay on track'

Consider for a moment that two people each want to lose weight. While one person may want to be able to walk up all four flights of stairs to his office at work without stopping along the way, that may mean nothing to the other person. Or say two women are both thinking of leaving their husbands. One may be thinking that she needs to get away from her husband's verbal harassment and occasional physical intimidation; the other may be feeling that she misses the emotional and physical intimacy that she used to have with her husband.

Indeed, research suggests that the more individualised our lists of reasons for wanting to change, the more likely we may be to stay on track. But I'm jumping ahead. Next comes a short questionnaire and then I'll explain everything.

TESTING, TESTING

Psychologists often ask people to complete questionnaires to gain useful insights into why they behave in the ways that they do. There are a handful of questionnaires to complete in this book and I'd like to introduce one of these to you right now.

The following questions ask you about specific events in your life and the way that you have gone about tackling different situations. I'll explain the relevance of the questions later, but for now, please trust me that your answers may help you to maximise your chances of successfully bringing about change in your life.

To enable you to get the most out of this chapter, you might like to pick up a pen and indicate your answers by choosing the appropriate number for each of the following questions:

	Never or seldom		Some-times		Very often
	1	2	3	4	5
1. Compared to most people, how often do you feel unable to get what you want out of life?					
2. Growing up, how often did you 'cross the line' by doing things that your parents would not tolerate?					

	1	2	3	4	5
3. How often have you accomplished things that got you 'psyched' or motivated to work even harder?					
4. How often did you obey rules and regulations that were established by your parents?					
5. How often do you feel that you have made progress towards being successful in your life?					
6. How often have you got into trouble by not being careful enough?					

All done?

I've adapted the six questions from a questionnaire created by a team of psychological investigators led by Tory Higgins at Columbia University in New York.[3] The questions actually give us two separate scores:

➡ To calculate your overall Avoidance score, add up the individual scores you gave yourself for questions 1, 2 and 6.

➡ Next, calculate your overall Approach score by adding up the individual scores for questions 3, 4 and 5.

Make a note of these two overall scores and I'll explain why they may help us.

CHASING BENEFITS AND EVADING ISSUES

People can often have quite different reasons for pursuing the same goals. Take a hypothetical husband and wife duo who both agree that they need to eat more vegetables, for example. John may decide to eat more greens because he thinks he will benefit by having more regular bowel movements and because he thinks it'll help him to lose some weight. Jane, on the other hand, may believe that eating greens will help her to avoid conditions such as high blood pressure and reduce the risk of illnesses such as heart disease and cancer.

Now John and Jane's individual motivations may at first glance seem quite similar, but psychologists would say that they're actually completely different. While John is pursuing benefits by eating more vegetables, Jane is dodging the possible negative consequences of *not* eating more vegetables.

That may sound like a purely semantic distinction of more interest to linguistics experts than the rest of us. But it turns out that it's a difference with useful repercussions for the way we motivate ourselves to introduce change into our lives.

And so we come to the science bit. Psychologists have for some years been investigating the idea of what they've called 'regulatory orientation' – whether people prefer to focus on the benefits of doing something or the downsides of *not* doing it when trying to change (or regulate) their behaviour. So John would be categorised as having an 'approach' regulatory orientation. He is setting out to modify his behaviour because he thinks he will reap benefits from doing so (in his case regular bowel movements and weight loss). In contrast, Jane has an 'avoidance' regulatory orientation. She and others like her may focus on the fact that *not* changing their behaviour might lead to negative consequences (in her case poor health or illness). These avoidance-focused individuals are therefore more likely to do things because they think that doing so will help them to elude certain downsides.

Let me illustrate the distinction with a couple of further examples. Suppose two people decide at the start of a New Year that they want to hit the gym. Someone who opts to exercise in order to stay fit and full of energy – i.e. focusing on the benefits – would be said to have more of an approach regulatory orientation. But a gym-goer who is afraid of putting on weight or who worries about the risk of osteoporosis – i.e. focusing on the drawbacks of *not* exercising regularly – would have an avoidance regulatory orientation.

I know two business people who showcase the distinction rather well too. Both are determined, ambitious would-be business moguls. They each run a thriving business: Srikumar works as a freelance web designer and Roderick as the managing partner in a small firm of physiotherapists. Both would like to grow their businesses further. But they each work hard and strive for results for almost the opposite reasons to each other.

Srikumar talks constantly about the benefits of working hard. To him, working hard and winning new clients allows him to earn more money. And that wealth allows him to buy the possessions, holidays and lifestyle that he desires. He focuses on wringing out every benefit and advantage of being successful – he has an approach regulatory orientation.

While Roderick works equally hard, he seems to do so for different reasons. I've known him a long time and he's only talked about it on a couple of occasions, but it's clear to me that he seeks to grow his business not so much because it will make him wealthy, but because he hopes that it will mean that he will never be poor. Even though many people would consider him to be fairly wealthy or at least comfortably well off, he's ultra-careful about what he spends too. In other words, he doesn't focus on the benefits of earning more but on preventing the downsides that *not* having enough money might bring.

By now you've probably realised that your Approach and Avoidance scores from the six questions above give you an indication of the relative strength of these two drives in your life. If your Approach score is much greater than your Avoidance score, that suggests that you're more motivated when you focus on the benefits of changing your behaviour and the positive consequences you might attain if you achieve your goals. You're probably someone who has more of an approach regulatory orientation.

However, if your Avoidance score dwarfs your Approach score, you may have more of an avoidance regulatory orientation. You may be more incentivised by focusing on the downsides, risks and negative consequences that might materialise should you *fail* to alter your behaviour.

Of course, that's all very well in theory. But how does that actually help us?

To unravel the answer to this question, allow me to walk you through a study conducted by Leona Tam, a Hong Kong-born

Chinese researcher who is currently a professor at Old Dominion University in Virginia in the United States. She and her fellow academics looked at how people's regulatory orientations affected their ability to change their snacking habits.

The investigators began by seeking out several hundred participants to answer questions (like the ones I posed to you above) to determine whether they were more oriented towards approach (i.e. accruing benefits) or avoidance (i.e. averting negative consequences). These participants were then divided into different groups.

Some participants were asked to read a paragraph that focused on the benefits of healthier eating as follows:

> According to nutrition experts, the most effective way to improve your snacking habit is to focus on the benefits of healthy snacking for you personally and to commit yourself to eating more healthy snacks.

Others were urged to focus on the downsides of unhealthy eating. These participants read a paragraph as follows:

> According to nutrition experts, the most effective way to improve your snacking habit is to focus on the drawbacks of unhealthy snacking for you personally and to commit yourself to eating more healthy snacks.

Reading the two paragraphs, I'm sure you will agree that the differences are fairly minor or even entirely inconsequential. But the results were far from trivial.

The participants were asked to keep food diaries for several days to establish what they actually ate. When their diaries were scrutinised, it turned out that those participants who had been given instructions consistent with their regulatory orientation had significantly healthier diets than both those who had been presented with instructions that went against their regulatory orientation.

For example participants with an avoidance regulatory orientation benefited more strongly when asked to direct their attention to the drawbacks of unhealthy eating (i.e. when they were given avoidance-focused instructions) than when asked to ponder the benefits of healthy eating.[4]

OVER TO YOU

To me, the research on regulatory orientation indicates the complexities of the human mind. All of us are not the same. We are motivated to change our behaviours for quite different reasons.

Some of us more naturally gravitate towards the positives, the upsides and benefits of behaving in certain ways. Others tend more easily to focus on the risks, the problems and negative consequences of *not* adopting those behaviours.

So what's your regulatory orientation? If your Approach score is higher than your Avoidance score, you might be wise to spend more time thinking about the benefits of the changes you'd like to make. If, on the other hand, your Avoidance score is higher than your Approach score, you may help yourself to keep on track by spending more time pondering the downsides and hazards of *not* changing and instead staying as you are.

If your Approach score is more or less the same as your Avoidance score (either the exact same or perhaps just one point higher or lower), then you have a fairly balanced regulatory orientation. This suggests that you can focus equally on both the upsides and benefits of change as well as the problems and drawbacks of not changing.

Perhaps another way of looking at regulatory orientation is that it's about whether we do things in life because we want to pursue success or sidestep failure. I often coach individuals on how to give more effective presentations, for example. I remember one client, whom I'll call Cynthia, from a few years ago who wanted to learn to give better presentations because she wanted to impress her clients, colleagues and bosses.

'The more people understand themselves and their orientations in life, the more they tend to succeed in achieving their goals'

She wanted to be noticed for all the right reasons so came to me to work on her presence and impact. She was wholly focused on pursuing success.

However, I worked with a different executive more recently, whom I'll call Marcello. He wanted to improve his presentation skills more because he was afraid of failure. His motivation stemmed less from wanting to impress and more from wanting to avoid looking stupid when standing up in front of his peers. So while Cynthia was more interested in the benefits of giving a good presentation, Marcello was more focused on the dangers of giving a poor presentation.

Anyway, I'm sure you get the point. The more people understand themselves and their orientations in life – either focusing on benefits or downsides as appropriate – the more they tend to succeed in achieving their goals.

ONWARDS AND UPWARDS

➡ To goad yourself into action, spend some time listing reasons as to why you might be yearning to change. Consider talking about them with friends and family too. Identifying your personal motivations for change may help you to translate your intentions into action.

➡ Remember from the study by Barbara Müller that people who come up with their own reasons for change are more likely to take the necessary action than people who are told the same reasons. So if you're looking to goad a friend or loved one to change, avoid nagging them by simply telling them why they should pursue a new job, take up a sport or whatever else you want them to do. Instead, keep asking them to come up with their own reasons why they might want to change.

➡ Consider whether you're someone who is focused more on the promotion of benefits or the prevention of drawbacks. In attempting to alter things about yourself or your life, are you hoping to amass benefits or to avoid problems? Bearing the distinction in mind may help you to establish more powerful goals.

➡ And remember there's a step-by-step guide to change at the back of this book, starting on page 237.

TWO

SETTING EFFECTIVE GOALS

'Achievable goals are the first step
to self improvement.'
J. K. Rowling

A buddy of mine from university, Liam, and his wife, Anna-Marie, are a tidy and well-presented couple in their late thirties who moved into a new home nearly a year ago. Like many couples, they had the choice of buying either a smaller house that was well maintained or a larger one in somewhat worse condition. They went for the latter, having decided that they wanted as many bedrooms as they could afford.

The house needs a lot of work. Most of the interior requires plastering again before they can paint it. The only bathroom in the two-storey house is a cold and damp room currently situated on the ground floor that can only be accessed through the kitchen, so Liam and Anna-Marie want to convert one of the upstairs bedrooms into a bathroom and turn the current bathroom into a utility room. What's more, there's a hole in the floor of one of the bedrooms – the floorboards are rotten and if you were to walk on the spot, you'd probably fall through the ceiling of the living room. And those are only *some* of the changes that they need to make to the house.

I always enjoy meeting Liam for lunch. He has the manic charm and dynamism of someone who should be a motivational speaker or a TV evangelist. On one occasion, I asked him when he was going to start the renovations.

'Soon,' he said.

The next time I saw him, I asked him again and he said, 'Soon.' Pretty much every time I met Liam – either on his own or with his wife – he flashed a goofy smile and said, 'Soon,' or 'I'll get round to it when I've got time.'

I actually stopped asking fairly recently because I could tell from the daggers that Anna-Marie was shooting him, and her terse jokes-that-weren't-jokes, that 'soon' was a moving deadline. To be fair, Liam's job keeps him very busy, but I suspect that he's also grown accustomed to living in a slightly shabby house – it doesn't bother him that much.

His reaction is particularly interesting from a psychological point of view. By saying that he will start the repair work 'soon', Liam is – either deliberately or, more probably, subconsciously – letting himself off the hook. If he said that he would 'plaster the spare bedroom this weekend' or 'rip out the bathroom by the end of September', those would be commitments that Anna-Marie, his friends and the rest of his family could hold him to. He'd undoubtedly feel the pressure and might actually start renovating his home.

'We are much less likely to achieve what we want when we are vague about our goals and intentions'

Whether we're planning a project to do with home improvement or personal improvement, the lesson is the same: we're more likely to take action when we make an overt pledge about what we'll do and when we'll do it. Research tells us that we are much less likely to achieve what we want when we are vague about our goals and intentions. So in this chapter, we're going to look at how to set goals that will give us the best shot of making the modifications we desire.

PLANNING TO SUCCEED

You may or may not wish to get fitter or lose weight. But weight reduction has become a massive topic of interest to psychologists and, by examining how researchers have successfully helped people to trim their waistlines, we will uncover how we might achieve our own goals too – whatever they might be.

Since 1980, obesity rates have tripled in many parts of the world including the UK, North America, China, the Middle East and Australia. The most recent World Health Organization study in 2003 estimated that over a *billion* adults are either overweight or obese.[5]

Many people find it tough to lose weight. Everywhere we look, we're assailed by opportunities to consume fast food and unhealthy snacks, which are usually loaded with saturated fat and sugar. It's often quicker and easier to buy an unhealthy (but oh so tasty) snack than to cook a healthy meal. And given that we're all working longer hours, who can blame us for wanting to relax afterwards with a beer or a glass of wine rather than hitting the gym?

Thankfully, behavioural scientists have discovered that certain tools can provide a greater incentive for people to lose weight. Aleksandra Luszczynska is a crusading health psychologist who has dedicated most of her career to investigating methods for helping people to live healthier lives. She's currently a professor at the University of Colorado, but when she was based in

England at the University of Sussex, she conducted a notable experiment with far-reaching consequences.

She began by recruiting a group of 25 women – all were either overweight or obese and keen to lose weight – for a study on weight reduction. The women were a diverse group aged from 18 to 76. Some had been overweight for only a year while others said they had been overweight for as long as they could remember – up to 40 years in some cases. You can imagine that these women were not just eager, but in some cases desperate to lose weight.

The participants were brought together to be weighed and given advice about which foods to eat and what kinds of physical exercise to perform. I'm sure you won't be surprised to hear that, amongst the recommendations, they were told to steer clear of sugary and fatty snacks and to eat more fruit and vegetables. Two months later, the women were gathered together again to see how much weight they had lost.

The women were given no additional support or guidance on how to lose weight, but after two months, they had on average shed 2.1 kg each. For many of the women, it was a promising start to getting into the shape they desired.

Here's the twist though. A second group of another 25 women had also been brought together and monitored over the same two months. And these women managed to lose a much more impressive 4.2 kg.[6]

Plainly, that's a big difference. The women in the second group had lost *twice* as much weight as those in the first. Put it this way: imagine if you could double the gains you make from any endeavour – or achieve them in half the time. That would be worthwhile, right?

How? Exactly what had the researchers taught these women?

Luszczynska and her fellow researchers had simply given the second group a booklet of additional written instructions and forms to fill in. I say booklet, but perhaps it would be more accurate to describe it as a pamphlet, as it only took the participants around 15 to 20 minutes to work their way through it. The instructions told the women:

> Planning when, where and what to eat as well as when, where and what exercises to perform has been found to help people translate their intentions into action. Using this form, make an exact plan of when and where you will eat the food you have selected and when, where and how you will exercise in the next 7 days.

The form then invited the participants to write detailed plans about six types of food (fruits, vegetables, meat, whole grain products, sweets and fatty foods). The form gave further instructions for each type of food. Here's an example of the one for vegetables:

> This is my plan of vegetable consumption for the next 7 days. During the next week, I plan to eat _____ (please, write down what type and amount of vegetables you plan to eat) at _____ (write down the time) in/at _____ (describe the situation/place where you plan to eat this food).

The women were encouraged to complete a daily plan for each of the six types of food. So that's 42 plans for a week. But the planning didn't stop there.

The researchers recognised that things don't always go right in people's lives. The best laid plans can get derailed by a friend offering to take us out for dinner or the gratification of a ready-made snack when we feel too hungry to cook. So the women were also told:

> Many situations may tempt you to eat something that you had not meant to. Make a plan about how you would react to these risky situations and fill in the form.

> I have my own plan that will help me to maintain my healthy diet. If I am hungry, then instead of eating an unhealthy snack I plan to _____ (write down what you plan to do). If someone offers me my favourite unhealthy food, in order not to eat it I plan to_____ (write down what you plan to do). If I meet with my friends or family over dinner, in order to eat healthy food I plan to _____ (write down what you plan to do).

As you can see, none of the advice is at all complex. In fact, on first glance it may even seem a bit patronising to ask people to write down exactly what they'll eat, and when and where.

But the point is that it made a difference. A huge difference. The women in the second group who were taught to complete these simple plans lost *twice* as much weight as those in the first group who tried to manage their weight through willpower alone.

FROM INTENTION TO IMPLEMENTATION

Reading this book, you probably have good intentions to change. But psychologists have ascertained that there's almost no link between the strength of people's intentions and the likelihood that they will actually make the change. Someone who's *desperate* to get a new job, leave a difficult personal situation, lose weight or whatever else is no more likely to succeed than someone who is only moderately motivated. Intentions such as, 'I will quit smoking,' 'I will become more organised,' or 'I will go to bed earlier and get more sleep every night,' do not automatically lead to action. For good reason, then, the old English proverb says that 'the road to hell is paved with good intentions'.

However, the good news is that specific intentions about what to do and when *do* make a difference. So rather than saying, 'I will quit smoking,' someone might decide, 'When I feel like a cigarette when I'm working from home, I will have a glass of water and do ten press-ups,' or 'When I feel the need for a cigarette when I'm driving, I will chew a piece of gum.'

One of my friends who was plagued by self-doubt and worry made a specific pledge to herself: 'Whenever I'm agitated, I will sing or hum a few lines of the Elvis Presley song "Can't Help Falling in Love"' (which was the first song that she and her husband danced to at their wedding). Since then, she has noticed on quite a few occasions that this simple promise has helped her to distance herself from her fears and calmed her frayed nerves.

Psychologists call these specific goals 'implementation intentions' – explicit action plans of how we propose to carry out our intentions. An enormous body of research tells us that making the effort to *write down* these detailed plans, these implementation intentions, is a big predictor of whether we will actually achieve our goals.

To give you a better idea of how such plans work, let me tell you about someone I'll call Marika, a client who came to me wanting to work on her attitude and behaviour towards her family and close friends. When we met, she said that she was content with her career achievements – she had an interesting and challenging job as a strategic planner at an advertising agency. However, a recent two-week holiday had helped her to reach an epiphany: she wasn't particularly happy in her personal life or, more precisely, with her attitude to life.

> 'Making the effort to *write down* detailed plans is a big predictor of whether we will actually achieve our goals'

Forty-five-year-old Marika – who, with her sleek chestnut hair and sturdy features, could pass for the sister or perhaps a cousin of the Hollywood star Sandra Bullock – explained that she had always been someone who found it easier to be critical and negative than to be upbeat and supportive. She tended to be the first to see the flaws in any project plan at work. But she was especially concerned that her attitude was having a corrosive effect on her relationships.

The main focus of our early discussions was her relationship with her husband. Having been together for over a decade, she was worried that they were drifting away from each other. When I asked her to sum up her overall goal, she said, 'I want to work on my relationship with my husband so that we can become like one of those close couples who still seem happy after thirty or forty years together.'

I asked her, 'What could you do that might help you to achieve that?'

After only a little thought, she said, 'I could be less critical. I'm always pointing out what he's forgotten to do. Even though he may have done five or six of the tasks I asked him to do, I tend to focus on the one that he didn't. I need to be less of a curmudgeon. I need to hold back my criticisms.'

'What else could you do?' I prompted.

'I could praise him more. He does so much that I take for granted. He notices when we run out of milk or laundry detergent and will pick some up on his way home and little things like that. I could thank him and show my appreciation for his efforts more.'

'What else?'

'I could take more time to show an interest in his work. When he tells me about his work, I'm usually cooking or sat at my laptop and have my back turned to him. I could listen better, ask a few more questions and comment more on what he's telling me than I normally do,' she said.

> **'Writing down commitments always seems to make our obligations so much more real'**

We carried on like this to spark further ideas. I then encouraged her to write them down so she wouldn't forget them. Writing down commitments always seems to make our obligations so much more real – almost like forming a written contract with ourselves. But the key point is this: by thinking about the different ways in which Marika could work on her relationship, she broke down her overall goal into a series of smaller, less daunting implementation intentions.

OVER TO YOU

People who simply wish or hope that their goals will materialise are likely to be disappointed. Dozens of studies have shown that people who write down their implementation intentions are more likely to attain their goals. And all it takes is a few minutes of thought on your part.

Begin by taking a fresh sheet of paper or opening up a new document on your computer and writing your goal at the top. So this may be something like, 'I will broaden my social circle and go out more this year,' 'I want to move to a new house away from the city,' or 'I will take better care of myself.'

Next, draw up a table as follows:

What will I do exactly and in detail?	*When* will I do it?

Then imagine that someone – perhaps a close friend, or me as your psychologist and coach – is asking you '*How* will you achieve your goal? Exactly *what* will you do to accomplish it?'

> Keep asking yourself those questions and jotting down all of the individual actions, the small steps you could take to achieve your overall goal. Think about where you might put a specific implementation intention into action as well as who else might be involved. The more specific and detailed each action you write down, the more likely you are to carry out – implement – your good intentions.

I remember emphasising the importance of having a detailed action plan to a talented client I'll call Tomas. A Lithuanian by birth who had studied at Vilnius University and gained a degree in political science, he came to me because he was desperate to get a more challenging job. He came to the UK several years ago wanting to get a job in political activism but, despite getting a handful of interviews, had been rejected every time. To keep alive his hopes of working in his chosen field, he had taken a part-time job as an unpaid volunteer at a charitable organisation involved in political campaigning. But to pay the bills, he was juggling two other part-time administrative jobs that were deeply unsatisfying.

When I first met him, I suspected that it wasn't a lack of qualifications or relevant experience that was holding him back, so much as that his English language skills weren't strong enough for employers to warrant giving him a chance; he used incorrect tenses, constructed his sentences in an unusual manner, and spoke haltingly in a strong accent.

When I gently told him what I thought he might work on, it would have been easy for Tomas to have made a broad resolution, such as, 'I will work on my English.' But *how* exactly? What *specific* steps would he take to work on his pronunciation, grammar and vocabulary?

So we devised a plan that broke his broad goal down into a number of individual, specific actions. The first draft of his implementation intention or action plan went along the lines of the following:

What will I do exactly and in detail?	When will I do it?
At work, ask colleagues to correct my English grammar and pronunciation. Tell them that I *want* to be criticised, otherwise I'll never learn.	Remind people at least once a week.
Start going out to drinks with (English-speaking) colleagues – particularly Paul, Alice, Chris.	Most likely Friday evenings.
Use Facebook and the Internet to find an English person who wants to learn Lithuanian or Russian in exchange for practising English with me.	End of week.
Find a club or social group (charity, five-a-side football team?) allowing me to mingle more with English people.	Make a decision by end of month.
Join in with or initiate conversations with colleagues about what we're watching on TV, for example.	When we first arrive into the office in the mornings and we're talking about what we did the previous evening.

In putting together your own plan, you might be wondering: how many individual implementation intentions is *enough*? The exact same question occurred to Amelie Wiedemann, one of the world's foremost experts in behaviour change at the Institute of Medical Psychology in Berlin, so let me talk you through one of her studies that was published in 2011.

Most governments around the world recommend that we eat a certain number of portions of fruits and vegetables. Even people who are slim and of healthy weight often need to eat more fruits and vegetables in order to ward off disease and stay healthy later in life. However, surveys consistently show that a large proportion of people simply don't eat enough carrots, apples, broccoli, tomatoes and the like.

Wiedemann and her team enrolled 478 volunteers to take part in their study, dividing them into six groups. The first group was taught the theory behind implementation intentions and asked to write down only one implementation intention. The second group generated two implementation intentions, and so on, with a fifth group being encouraged to write out five separate implementation intentions. The sixth group was not taught about implementation intentions – these participants acted as a control group and simply completed questionnaires about their dietary habits.

When the researchers followed up on the groups and asked them about their fruit and vegetable consumption, they found that it was only the groups that had generated four or five of these 'what and when' plans that had benefited. The groups that had been asked to come up with only one, two or even three implementation intentions were eating no more fruits and vegetables than the control group that hadn't been taught the skill of forming implementation intentions at all.[7]

This doesn't necessarily mean that generating two or three implementation intentions has *no* benefit. It may be that the effect was too small for the researchers to measure in this study. But the point is that the number of these individual action plans we come up with seems to matter. If we want to make the most of our implementation intention plans, we might do well to aim for at least four or five separate actions.

'To make the most of our implementation intention plans, we might do well to aim for at least four or five separate actions'

It's a shame that the research team didn't have further groups that were asked to write out six, seven, eight, ten, a dozen or more implementation interventions. I suspect that it could be even more advantageous to write out greater numbers of actions, but we can't say for certain yet.

OVERCOMING OBSTACLES

Let's pause for a moment to think about what an implementation intention actually is. It represents how we'd like to behave when our affairs are on track, under control and going to plan. It's a best-case scenario that describes our intended action *when things are going well.*

However, we know that things don't always go well. Problems crop up. Schedules can suddenly change. People may let us down. Things can go awry and we may find ourselves in a predicament that may not be conducive to achieving our goals.

For example, say you're trying to get fitter. At the start of the week, you decide that you would like to go for a run on Thursday evening after work. But just as you're on the way home, the skies loom dark with ominous-looking clouds. And by the time you get home, the thunder is booming overhead and torrents of rain are falling from the heavens. The rain is so heavy and the visibility so poor that you're worried about the possibility of being hit by a car. It's definitely not the right time to go for a run.

What then? You might be tempted to slump in front of the TV. But if you had a back-up plan – something as simple perhaps as running up and down the stairs to your apartment a dozen times – you might be able to do some exercise despite the weather and still work towards your goal of getting fitter.

Or suppose you're trying to cut down the number of cigarettes you smoke. It's all very well deciding that you're going to halve the number of times you light up. But what if a friend should offer you a cigarette unexpectedly? How will you resist the temptation? Again, having a contingency plan – perhaps to have a pack of mints to suck – might stop you from giving in to a moment of weakness.

These back-up or contingency plans are called *coping intentions* by psychologists. If you look back at the instructions that Aleksandra Luszczynska used in her weight-loss study at the University of Sussex (on page 46), you'll notice that the participants were also asked to make plans about the 'risky situations' that might tempt them to overeat.

Again, research tells us that people who think ahead about the likely hurdles they might face – and the actions they would take when faced with those obstacles – are more likely to succeed in achieving their goals.[8]

'Thinking ahead about the probable complications may allow us to take a small detour rather than be derailed entirely'

Of course, we can't predict all of the problems or barriers that may thwart us from achieving our goals. But thinking ahead about the handful of most probable complications may allow us to take a small detour (but still stay on track to achieving our goals) rather than be derailed entirely.

Let's reflect on how this might work in practice by thinking about Brian, a hypothetical man in his thirties who is trying to drink less alcohol because he realises that he is drinking far more than is healthy. Of course, he begins by listing appropriate implementation intentions. Once he's done that, though, he thinks about the main barriers and identifies three main worries:

➡ 'My friend Alan – he'll laugh at me and try to goad me into drinking whenever we're out at a bar or having dinner.'

➡ 'Sitting down for dinner with my wife Rachel. We usually open a bottle of wine most nights of the week. After a couple of glasses, we may only have a third of the bottle left over and Rachel will encourage me to finish it rather than let it go off.'

➡ 'Friday night drinks with friends from work. There's a lot of peer pressure to keep drinking and drinking and to stay until the end of the evening.'

Taking each of these in turn, Brian draws up a table with the headings 'barriers' and 'tactics' at the top of the two columns. He fills it out as follows:

Barriers	Tactics
Alan laughing at me and goading me into drinking.	I'll laugh with him, let him have his joke and agree that I'm turning into a big wimp. Once I've told him that he wins, I will still order a non-alcoholic drink.
Rachel encouraging me to finish off a bottle of wine.	I need to buy one of those vacuum wine stoppers so that we can put the bottle back in the fridge and finish it off the next evening.
Drinking with colleagues after work on Friday evenings.	I'll say that I have to drive to pick Rachel up from the station later, and I can only drink one alcoholic drink so that I'm not over the limit.

OVER TO YOU

By now you may have written up a list of your implementation intentions – a list of the actions you'll take, and when you intend to take them, when things are going well. That's a great start – but now, on a fresh sheet of paper, again write your goal at the top. So it might be, 'I want to get a promotion within the next twelve months,' 'I want to get ready to have a baby,' or 'I want to eat less meat and more vegetables.'

Next, draw a line down the centre of the page and write the words 'barriers' at the top of the left-hand column and 'tactics' on the right-hand side.

Barriers	Tactics

Then try to list likely obstacles, problems, complications and difficult situations down the left-hand side of the page. In most studies, researchers try to encourage participants to list at least three or five barriers that they might encounter.

Once you've done that, try to think of tactics you could use to reduce the impact of those barriers. Even better, how might you evade each obstacle or ordeal entirely?

For example, reflect on the impact of the following hurdles in your particular situation:

➡ People – which individuals are likely to be least supportive or even downright obstructive?

➡ Unexpected appointments or social engagements – what will you do when, for example, you need to stay late at work or friends suggest meeting up at short notice?

➡ Times of day – are there any times of day that are riskiest for succumbing to temptation? If you can identify when you're most likely to falter, you can make plans to avoid letting yourself down.

➡ Weather – what impact might inclement weather have on your goals?

➡ Technology/computer issues – what technology are you relying on? And what's your back-up if it shouldn't be working?

➡ Tiredness/laziness – if you are too exhausted or simply not in the mood to pursue your goals, how might you make up for it either later that day or the next day?

Of course, those are only some of the most common snags that people face. What are the main issues that *you* may face?

A client of mine named Arjun once came to me for support in making a career shift. He had started his career as a sales assistant at a high-street electronics chain but quickly worked his way up. Not yet 30 years of age, he was already a store manager for one of the chain's larger stores.

It wasn't what he wanted to do, though, and he sought my assistance to discover a more fulfilling career path. With only a little guidance, he decided that he wanted to retrain as an independent financial advisor. It would cost him several thousands of pounds and he would need to take over half a dozen exams, but he felt that it would be both intellectually satisfying as well as interpersonally interesting to help people with their financial planning.

After a few months of his studies, we met for a review session and he told me that he had the best intentions to hunker down and study, but that things often got in the way. I explained the theory behind coping intentions and suggested that we discuss barriers and suitable tactics for dealing with them. Here are just a few that he identified:

Barriers	Tactics
Favourite show on TV.	Record the show to watch AFTER I've done a few hours of studying.
Feeling lazy after work.	Get up an hour earlier in the morning to do an hour of study before I go to work.
Feeling tired after dinner.	Have a snack when I first get home while the kids have their dinner to keep me going. Then [wife] Priyanka and I will have dinner AFTER I've studied.

Clearly, none of the items on Arjun's list are intellectually challenging. The concept of coping intentions isn't complicated. It's not that we don't comprehend what to do – it's that we often struggle to put our intentions into practice. Happily, we can trust what the science tells us. The simple act of writing out a list of coping intentions significantly boosts the odds that we will achieve our goals.

GETTING STARTED

If you're deadly serious about changing your life or circumstances, I hope that you'll put into practice the notion of these 'what and when' or implementation intention plans. There's robust science endorsing their effectiveness. Putting it simply: *they work*.

I know that some readers will skip on to the next chapter in the belief that *understanding* the concepts of implementation intentions and coping intentions will be enough. But sadly that's not how it seems to work. I know from past books I've written that the many readers who get the results are the ones who actually put pen to paper or fingers to keyboard.

This isn't an instant fix. Setting goals, writing out implementation intentions and then figuring out appropriate coping implementations takes time – perhaps even an hour or two. To put it into context, there are 168 hours in a week and 8,760 hours in a year. What's a couple of hours? Think about the results you might achieve.

As a final example, consider an experiment led by psychologist Dominique Morisano at McGill University in Montreal. Her research team recruited nearly 100 struggling students to see if goal setting and planning could improve their grades. When I say that these students were struggling, many of them had been placed on what North American universities call academic probation – i.e. having performed so poorly that they were in danger of being dismissed from university. Half of the students spent two and a half hours writing out their goals and implementation intention plans; the other half were assigned to a control condition and asked to spend a comparable amount of time writing about positive past experiences. Four months later, the students who'd been taught to write out their plans had improved their grades significantly; the other students hadn't got any better.[9]

'Readers who get the results are the ones who actually put pen to paper or fingers to keyboard'

The planning worked – it delivered results. But the point is: it took *two and a half hours* of *writing and planning*. Effective planning can't be done in the space of mere minutes or simply worked out in our heads. It takes concentration and careful consideration to figure out the details. Will you invest the time to work out your personal change plan?

ONWARDS AND UPWARDS

➡ Remember that having good intentions – even really strong ones – doesn't always help people to change. Intentions are often too vague to help people to actually institute changes in their lives.

➡ Lay the groundwork for putting your intentions into action by working out at least four or five different 'implementation intentions'. The formula for success is simple: think about *what* you'll do, *where* you might do it, *who* else you could involve and *when* you'll do it.

➡ In addition, make time to work out the major barriers that might prevent you from achieving your goals. By mapping out relevant 'coping intentions', you will help yourself to avoid getting derailed by unexpected problems.

➡ To give yourself the very best chance of making change happen in your life, see the additional practical tips in The Change Manifesto section at the back of this book (which starts on page 237).

THREE

BOOSTING OUR WILL TO SUCCEED

'I can resist anything but temptation.'
Oscar Wilde

Yvonne is an easy-going, vivacious friend of mine with fiery red hair and a round face that is always immaculately made up to bring out her green eyes. Now in her late forties, she embarked on a new relationship less than a year ago with a man more than 10 years younger. She is a passionate cook and, especially in the early months of the relationship, cooked lots of lavish meals for the two of them. As such, both she and her new partner have put on quite a bit of weight. She asked me for advice and I've been helping her to lose weight on an informal basis. Whenever we get together, she chatters as excitedly about her favourite TV shows as her love life, but eventually we talk a little about her goals, her implementation intentions and what she's managed to achieve.

A couple of weekends ago, she had lunch with a group of friends at a seafood restaurant in the centre of the city. She ordered a starter of grilled vegetables, followed by a whole sea bream roasted with garlic, thyme and white wine for her main course, with a portion of steamed broccoli on the side. Close to a perfect healthy meal.

After savouring their two courses at a leisurely pace, Yvonne and her companions decided that two courses were plenty so they skipped dessert. Privately, she was pleased that they weren't eating dessert. Not having unnecessary calories was definitely a good thing!

The friends weren't ready for the afternoon to end and trotted down the street to a cafe where they could linger and chat. Queuing to place their orders for coffee at the counter, they couldn't help but notice glass bell jars displayed prominently at eye level containing mouth-watering pastries, muffins and cakes.

And that's how Yvonne ended up devouring a thick wedge of dark- and white-chocolate cheesecake. Despite the fact she'd been perfectly satisfied by her relatively healthy two-course meal – and in spite of her best intentions not to eat anything else – she gave in to temptation.

This is probably not an unfamiliar scenario. We've all experienced occasions when our resolve has crumbled, when our willpower hasn't been enough. Even when we decide that we're definitely *not* going to do something – lose our temper, drink too much at a party or wolf down an entire bowl of peanuts – we can find our willpower betraying us. The same goes when we decide that we're definitely going to do something positive – go to the gym, ask someone out or adopt a more cheery attitude on life. Tiredness, stress and worry, or even simple laziness can derail our best intentions and even our best implementation intentions.

The good news is that help is at hand. Psychologists have spent nearly 40 years investigating willpower and the methods we can use to boost it.

TESTING YOUR WILLPOWER

Before I explain what willpower is and how we can make the best of it, let me ask you a question. How good are *you* at resisting temptation and staying in control? Here's a question-naire called the Self-Control Scale (SCS). You might like to take the test before reading on.

Using the scale provided, please indicate how much each of the following statements reflects how you typically are.

	1 Not at all	2	3	4	5 Very much
1. I am good at resisting temptation.					
2. I have a hard time breaking bad habits.					
3. I am lazy.					
4. I say inappropriate things.					
5. I do certain things that are bad for me, if they are fun.					
6. I refuse things that are bad for me.					
7. I wish I had more self-discipline.					
8. People would say that I have iron self-discipline.					
9. Pleasure and fun sometimes keep me from getting work done.					
10. I have trouble concentrating.					

	1 Not at all	2	3	4	5 Very much
11. I am able to work effectively towards long-term goals.					
12. Sometimes I can't stop myself from doing something, even if I know it is wrong.					
13. I often act without thinking through all the alternatives.					

To calculate your total score, begin by adding up the individual scores for statements 1, 6, 8 and 11. For the other statements, you will need to reverse each individual score by subtracting it from 6. For example, if you gave yourself a score of '1' for one of the statements, then 6 minus 1 equals 5.

So for statements 2, 3, 4, 5, 7, 9, 10, 12 and 13, reverse your scores before adding them up. You might want to check your scores to make sure you haven't made a mistake!

The Self-Control Scale is the brainchild of an elite research team headed by June Tangney, a professor of psychology at George Mason University in Virginia with more than 25 years' experience of investigating people's morals and emotions. When the researchers invited over 600 people to complete the SCS, they found that higher self-control scores predicted all manner of positive outcomes. People who scored higher for self-restraint and willpower generally had higher scholastic grades. They also had higher self-esteem, were emotionally better adjusted, and less likely to suffer from eating disorders or to abuse alcohol. High scorers on the SCS even reported that they had more cohesive relationships with their families; they experienced less conflict interpersonally too.

You may be wondering: what's a high score, a low score, or even an average score? When Tangney and her fellow investigators looked at their data, they found that the average score on the SCS was around 39.[10]

A score of 33 or less would put you in the bottom 25 per cent as compared with most people. In other words, three out of four people would have higher levels of self-control and willpower than you. On the other hand, a score of 45 or more would put you in the top 25 per cent.

But how does that help us? What does it all mean?

DELVING INTO THE HUMAN MIND

If you've ever said, 'I wish I could be more disciplined,' or 'I can't seem to help it,' you're not alone. Sometimes it feels like, if we only had a little more willpower, we'd be able to carve out precisely the lives we long for. But what is willpower exactly?

To answer the question, we need to compare and contrast the behaviour of most animals with that of the particular animal known as Homo sapiens, the human being. If you think about most animals – dogs, cats, birds, elephants, pandas and just about all living beasts that walk, fly, swim or crawl on this planet

– we talk about their *animal* nature. When they're hungry or thirsty, they eat or drink. When their bowels or bladders are full, they defecate or urinate. When they see a predator, they either flee or get ready to fight. When they encounter a fine specimen of the opposite sex, they mate. That's what animals do.

And that's what humans do *some* of the time too. We generally eat when we're hungry and drink when we're thirsty. We relieve ourselves throughout the day. We run away when we're frightened or get into brawls when we feel threatened – albeit mostly verbal altercations, but sometimes physical ones too. And most healthy adults take a great interest when the opportunity for sex arises.

But we humans don't always act on our desires, our basic natures. When we're hungry, we can *decide* not to eat. When we're thirsty, we can *choose* to wait for many hours before drinking. When we feel threatened, we can opt to respond calmly and rationally rather than letting our fight or flight response kick in. And sure, we may be impassioned and inflamed by the idea of sex, but we don't jump on the nearest partner available and rut in public like mere *animals*.

The fact that we have an animal side but can decide to override it has led many psychologists to believe that the human mind is made up of two competing systems.[11] One of these is a 'hot' system that may have been passed down to us from our animal ancestors many millions of years ago. This hot system is a set of instincts and simple reflexes – an autopilot – governed by our emotions and our biological needs. It generates feelings and impulses about what to do from moment to moment. When we feel afraid, hungry, tired, angry, sad, disgusted or whatever else, this hot system drives us to take immediate action to deal with the situation and meet our most basic needs.

On the other hand, we also have a 'cool' system that we humans probably developed much more recently in evolutionary terms – perhaps only hundreds or even tens of thousands of years ago. This cool system is based on rational thought. It allows us to weigh up our options and, if necessary, consciously overrule the impulses and actions that our hot systems urge us towards. When we realise that our feelings and instincts may be driving us towards inappropriate behaviour, our cool system allows us to override them – to pull rank and take manual control, if you will. And it's the circuitry within this so-called cool system that allows us to exercise self-control, restraint and willpower over our biological impulses; it gives humans the capacity above all other animals to make and carry out plans, behave responsibly, and do what's right and good for us in the long run rather than what feels right in the here-and-now.

So even though our bodies may crave food, we can rationally decide not to indulge because we yearn to lose weight or because we want to finish a report at work before we eat. Even though we may sometimes wish we could yell at an annoying colleague, we can reject the urge and choose to walk away from the situation. And when we're feeling tired, we can choose to go to the gym, study for an exam, clean the house or do whatever else would be more beneficial. In each instance, we can use our cool system – our willpower – to override our more capricious natures; we can choose to behave in ways that might ultimately help us to achieve our longer-term goals.

But there's a catch – and one that probably won't surprise you. Our ability to exercise self-control is limited. Willpower may be a finite resource, like a tank of fuel. The more temptations

'Willpower may be a finite resource, like a tank of fuel'

we have to resist, the more swiftly we burn through our reserves. And when we run out . . . that's when our hot system seizes control and our best intentions may look very precarious indeed.

UNDERSTANDING THE LIMITS OF WILLPOWER

Why do psychologists believe that willpower is a limited resource?

Scientists have done some cunning experiments over the years, which often involve subjecting experimental volunteers to various forms of torment. All in the interests of science, of course!

Research psychologist Mark Muraven has spent more than a decade investigating the concept of willpower, its limitations and the methods we can deploy to boost it – an interest that developed when he was an undergraduate with a self-confessed weakness for sugary snacks. He's currently a professor of psychology and director of the Self-Control in Life Laboratory at the University of Albany in New York, but let's begin by stepping back in time to 1998, when he was just an enthusiastic young protégé working on a master's thesis in psychology at Case Western Reserve University in Ohio.

Muraven and his older mentors began their seminal study by enticing – quite literally, as we shall see – a group of students to take part in what they told their volunteers was to be a somewhat quirky experiment on the effects of different food types on problem solving. As such, the unfortunate participants had been told not to eat anything for three hours before the investigation to make sure that they were hungry.

Each participant arrived individually and was brought into a testing room and sat at a table with a plate of freshly baked chocolate-chip cookies and a bowl filled with red-and-white radishes. The experimenter had filled the testing room with the scent of the freshly baked cookies, so it was impossible to miss them.

The experimenter invited half of the participants to eat a couple of cookies, which they all did. You can imagine that they didn't need much coaxing.

Unfortunately, the other half of the group were told to refrain from eating any of the cookies. No, not a single one. To add insult to injury, the experimenter invited them to fill their bellies with as many radishes as they liked.

You can imagine the disappointment on the faces of the participants who were told that they wouldn't be allowed any cookies. Think how you'd feel if you were hungry and confronted with delicious-looking cookies. You'd have to avoid thinking about the juicy chocolate chunks and the just-baked dough. You'd have to try to shut out the intoxicatingly delicious aroma. Like I said, a minor form of torture!

The experimenter then explained the problem-solving task to the participants. You can have a go for yourself if you like. The task requires you to trace a geometric figure – i.e. to recreate the whole shape – without retracing any lines and without lifting your pen from the paper. If you've got some spare sheets of paper handy, you can give the one below a go. The solution is on page 78, so don't turn over until you've either worked it out or decided to give up.

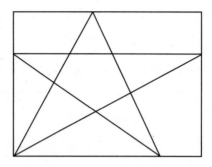

But here's the twist to the experiment. The participants were actually given an unsolvable conundrum – one in which it's impossible to recreate the whole figure without either lifting your pen off the page or retracing a line.

Here's an example of an unsolvable shape; the extra line on the right-hand side means it can't be done. But the hapless participants didn't know that it couldn't be done, and in fact the researchers were actually interested in seeing how long the participants would persist at an intractable problem.

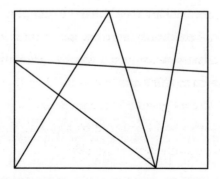

The researchers left the participants with the unsolvable task and timed how long it took for each of them to declare defeat. On average, the participants who had been allowed to sample the chocolate-chip cookies lasted 18.90 minutes before giving up. But the unfortunate participants who had been forbidden from eating the cookies gave up after less than half as long – they only lasted 8.35 minutes on average.[12]

It seemed that *not* eating a tempting food had made it harder for the participants to persist with the frustrating problem. More broadly, the study suggests that exercising self-restraint in any area of our lives may make it more difficult to persevere with even different, unrelated tasks.

In fact, the same pattern has been identified time and again. Just for fun, imagine that you're a participant in an experiment. I want you to spend 60 seconds *not* thinking about a white bear. Go on. Close your eyes and give it a go – 60 seconds thinking about anything you like except the size and lumbering, furry shape of a white bear.

Difficult, right?

Indeed, volunteers in another experiment were separated into two groups. The researchers – led by our impresario Mark Muraven again – told the first group *not* to think about a white bear; the researchers mentioned a white bear to a second group and allowed them to think about it as much as they liked. When both groups were all given a subsequent problem-solving task, the volunteers who had been told to avoid all thoughts of the white bear gave up much more quickly.

In yet another study, participants who were directed not to show any emotion on their faces while watching an upsetting film actually exhibited less physical grip strength than participants who were allowed to express their emotions normally.[13] And in a final study, researchers found that people who were required to show more self-restraint during the day went on to drink more alcohol that evening.[14]

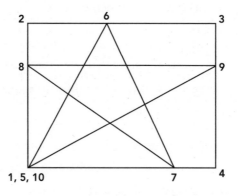

Psychological detectives like Muraven and others have therefore come to the conclusion that willpower is a limited resource, like energy or strength. When you lift a really heavy weight with your biceps, your arm gets tired and you can't lift another heavy weight straight away.

In the same way, when we draw upon our willpower, we temporarily exhaust our reserves. When we override our natural impulses, we may find it harder to forgo other indulgences or persist with even totally unrelated tasks later in the day – they all draw upon the same well of energy. In psychologists' parlance, the breakdown of self-control is sometimes called 'ego depletion' – a reduction in our ability to be rational and do what's in our own long-term interest.[15]

When we say no to dessert at lunchtime, we may find it harder to motivate ourselves to do some studying later that evening. When we spend a couple of hours pretending we like someone – a boss, the in-laws, a tricky client – whom we secretly despise, we may find it tougher to resist making an impulse purchase on the way home. Or when we stop ourselves from shouting at a colleague for a massively stupid mistake at work, we may become more irritable and end up taking it out on a loved one later on. The more demands we're under – both physically and emotionally – during the day, the more likely we are to run out of willpower later.

> 'The more demands we're under during the day, the more likely we are to run out of willpower later'

OVER TO YOU (PART I)

The discovery that willpower – the force or energy we use to restrain our impulses and emotions in order to persevere with our nobler goals – is a limited resource suggests that we can help ourselves to stick with our goals by making our environments as free from temptation as possible. Let's take weight loss as an example. Say you keep a sugary or fatty snack – perhaps your favourite cakes, muffins or biscuits – in a glass jar in the kitchen. Every time you traipse through the kitchen, you'll see the jar and will need to use up some of your precious willpower reserves to stop from helping your-self to one. If you put the jar into a hard-to-reach cupboard, though, you may be able to save some of your willpower because you won't see it all of the time. Better still, empty the jar entirely. Throw out the biscuits and you won't get tempted at all.

One of the goals I've set myself is to write one book a year. When I initially began writing in earnest a few years ago, I found myself easily distracted by what was going on outside. When I saw movement through the window, I automatically looked up – forcing me to use some of my scarce willpower when focusing on my work again. Likewise, when I saw movement through the open door to the office, I often looked that way too, wondering what was happening. My solution: move my desk. I now sit facing a boring, cream-coloured corner of the room. Both the window and door are behind me, which means I avoid more distractions and can save my willpower for the stuff that really matters.

Make no mistake: eliminating and removing temptations entirely is a better strategy for change than having to resist temptations constantly. What might you do to ensure your environment helps you to stick with the modifications you want to make?

OVER TO YOU (PART II)

The research actually suggests *two* momentous conclusions, so I thought I'd discuss them separately to ensure neither gets lost.

The fact that willpower can be depleted by exertions in different areas of our lives suggests that we should (ideally) aim to alter only one thing at a time. If we're trying to make a major improvement in one area, we might do well to keep the other parts stress free. Of course, life doesn't always work out so perfectly, but it's certainly an aspiration worth bearing in mind.

Say you're trying to keep your emotions in check so that you don't feel agitated so much of the time. To give yourself the best chance of success, don't take on a stressful project at work or decide to confront a loved one about problems that are making you unhappy alongside this new goal. If you use up your willpower on the work project or the confrontation at home, you will have less motivational fuel to keep your worries at bay.

Or if you wish to commit to studying for a new qualification, again try to hold off on other big changes. Avoid moving house and trying to adopt a more positive attitude at the same time, for instance.

Even if you're trying to make a series of smaller tweaks such as reading fewer trashy magazines or cutting down on the amount of salt you eat, avoid doing them all at once. If you can, stagger them. Get one habit sorted before you move on to the next.

At the start of the year, I went to a friend's party where I met a spirited and extremely talkative woman. Gesticulating with a glass of wine in her hand, she proceeded to tell me about her multiple New Year's resolutions: she hankered after a brand new job that would – in her words – 'fulfil her soul', cook a new recipe every week, read a work of non-fiction every month, take capoeira classes, start a photography blog . . . I can't actually remember everything she wanted to do because there was so much of it.

I didn't feel that I knew her well enough to offer her unsoli-cited advice – people don't always want to hear the unvarnished truth, especially if they didn't ask for it. But at the back of my mind I wanted to say that she would be better off staggering each phase of her ambitious life overhaul rather than trying to do it all at once.

I've not crossed paths with her since but I'm pretty sure I can guess what happened. We only have limited amounts of will-power. And dividing it between a half-dozen different goals means we may have less to invest in each than we would if we tackled each one individually. As a consequence, I'm almost certain that her efforts will by now have fizzled out.

TRAINING OUR WILLPOWER

I can't overstate the importance of willpower in our lives – it's the fuel that allows us to change. Think of it this way: every single time we exercise willpower, we are making a small change in our lives. Each act of self-control deflects us from our animal-istic urges in favour of our longer-term aspirations. Over time, the small alterations add up. And they keep adding up until we might suddenly find that we've accomplished the bigger changes we were pursuing.

In theory, if we only had more willpower, we'd all be able to improve our health – eating properly, exercising more, drinking less alcohol, and so on. We'd work harder, be more product-ive and contribute more not only to the organisations we work for but also to the economy in general. We could keep our emotions in check and become the people we want to be. In fact, we could say goodbye to laziness and keep just about every promise that we make.

Here's the best bit, though: the analogy about willpower being like a muscle is a cause for celebration too. Just as we can train a muscle to grow stronger through regular exercise, it so happens that we can increase our self-control. We can stoke our resolve and improve our ability to restrain detrimental impulses and unhealthy desires. *We can change.*

'Just as we can train a muscle to grow stronger through regular exercise, it so happens that we can increase our self-control'

We encountered über-researcher Mark Muraven earlier, and thankfully he hasn't only been documenting instances in which we exhibit failures of willpower. In his latest research, he has found that he has been able to enhance people's willpower too.

In one of these more recent studies, he recruited over 100 smokers into a trial, telling them that he would help them to enhance their willpower to give them the best shot at giving up smoking. Kicking off the experiment, he divided his participants into three groups. Two were taught willpower training exercises, while a third, control group was requested only to keep a diary of when they resisted temptation. Critically, the participants in this control group were not asked to actually resist temptation.

After only two weeks of training, the participants in all three groups were told to stop smoking – just like that, with no nicotine patches or even advice on how best to quit. What Muraven wanted to know was how long it took for the participants to experience their first lapse, to give in and have a cigarette again. And to check that none of the participants was lying about whether they had lapsed or not, he tested their breath biochemically for carbon monoxide!

The participants in the control group only lasted six days on average. Remember that even though they had been asked to keep a diary about when they had resisted temptation, they hadn't actually been asked to exercise any self-control.

The participants in the other two groups lasted *twice as long*, 12 days on average, before they gave into temptation to have a cigarette again. How? What miraculous techniques had Muraven taught them?

Thing is, this so-called willpower training involved hardly any work at all. It was so easy that the instructions can be explained in just a few sentences.

Both of the experimental groups had been asked to practise small acts of self-restraint. One group was instructed to cut out all sugary snacks for two weeks. The other group was ordered to squeeze a handgrip every day for the 14 days with a view to developing their physical endurance.[16]

'Willpower isn't something that is fixed. We can deepen our reserves of this vital fuel'

The study proved that training on one task can help to boost willpower in other areas of our lives. Cutting out sugar helped smokers to refrain from smoking for longer. So did squeezing a hand grip for a couple of minutes every day.

The wider implications of the study are monumental. Will-power isn't something that is fixed. We can deepen our reserves of this vital fuel. We can train ourselves to become more self-disciplined. We can improve our ability to restrain our some-times unhealthy desires and impulses. No longer will we let ourselves off the hook by saying things like, 'I'm just not very good at sticking with things,' or 'I can't help myself.'

Performing even modest acts of self-restraint can hone our overall willpower. And that may help us to tackle the bigger modifications we want to make in our lives. So no matter what you scored on the Self-Control Scale (SCS) earlier in this chapter, you can improve on it further.

OVER TO YOU

Let me repeat the lesson: performing small acts of self-control in *any* area of our lives can help us to increase the total amount of willpower we have. The results come rela-tively swiftly too: Mark Muraven's participants trained for a mere two weeks – that's nothing, right?

Suppose the transformation you want to make in your life relates to your emotions – to avoid slumps into depression or outbursts of anger, for example. *Before* you embark on this change, a good way to build up your reserves of willpower might be to train your self-control in some other area of your life, say by cutting certain things out of your diet – caffeine or chips perhaps. Once you've done that for a couple of weeks, that alone might boost your willpower and subsequent abil-ity to rein in your emotions.

Another example: if you want to improve your study skills so that you can gain a qualification and get a new job, perhaps get used to exerting more control in your life by regularly monitoring your posture and sitting more upright during meetings and even social engagements. Or decide to watch fewer hours of television every week. Or keep a diary monitoring the number of critical comments you make every day with a view to becoming more positive. Or put some money aside into a savings account every week.

Your options are endless. The only question is, what minor feats of self-restraint might *you* introduce into your life?

GIVING YOUR WILLPOWER
AN INSTANT BOOST

Okay, it's all very well being able to train up our willpower. But what if we need even more willpower for a particularly formidable challenge? Maybe you're going to a party where you know there'll be tables laden with unhealthy but mouth-watering pastries and cakes. Or you're going to a lengthy meeting with an important customer who happens to be one of the most obnoxious and argumentative people you've ever met.

Of course, there's no magic bullet, no miraculous elixir that will fortify our willpower forever. However, we do have a next best thing. Brandon Schmeichel, a relatively young but already highly decorated psychologist at Texas A&M University, and a colleague ran a series of experiments showing that we can boost our willpower without weeks of training for the occasions on which we need it. All it takes is a few minutes of quiet thinking alone with a pen and paper.

Again, the unfortunate volunteers were subjected to minor forms of torture. In one experiment, for example, the researchers tested their volunteers' pain thresholds by asking them to thrust their hands into icy cold water and to keep them there for as long as possible.

If you were to plunge your hand into freezing water, your immediate instinct would be to pull it out. Even though it's not actually dangerous, it's extremely uncomfortable and ultimately completely intolerable. It would require an act of willpower on your part to override the urge to lift your hand out. So it's a beautiful test of staying power.

When the merciless researchers timed their subjects, they observed that one group lasted only 27 seconds. But a second group lasted over a minute; they had twice as much willpower. How?

Before the test, the experimenters separated their participants into two randomly chosen groups. Both groups were shown a list of 11 values and personal characteristics and asked to rank them in order of personal importance. For example, many people listed 'relations with friends and family' as being amongst their top three or four values; some felt that 'physical attractiveness' was important while others rated 'creativity' more highly.

Next, all of the participants spent six minutes writing a short essay explaining why one of their values was so central to their lives. As part of their essays, the participants were also asked to describe an event or point in the past when the value had been particularly important.

The group who on average lasted only 27 seconds had been asked to write about their seventh most important value – i.e. one that was really only of middling importance to them. But the group who had on average lasted twice as long had been asked to write about their number one, top-ranked value. Writing about a crucial value had boosted their staying power.

In the same way, capturing *our* thoughts about an important value – something that we truly treasure – may boost our resolve too. Writing about, for example, the importance of family, career, religion, freedom or anything else that we cherish deeply may be useful when we need to perform a task that involves discomfort, such as standing up to a bullying colleague or working out at the gym.

And it has to be a value that is significant and meaningful to each of us as individuals. So what's of most importance to you may be different to the values that even your closest friends or family cherish. To prove this point, Schmeichel and his colleagues ran another experiment in which they called upon volunteers to write about either one of their own values or a value that might be important to someone else – specifically Bill Gates, the founder of software giant Microsoft and the world's richest man. The researchers measured willpower this time by asking the participants to persist with a series of increasingly gruelling word puzzles until they got too frustrated and gave up. Again, it was only the participants who had written about their own value who gained a boost to their persistence.[17]

When we want to stay on track – perhaps to study for an exam or stay focused on a challenging task at work – it seems that writing about one of our fundamental values may help us to stick with things for longer. Writing about someone else's value seems to have little benefit for our own willpower.

OVER TO YOU

We all have different priorities in life, but what are yours? To supercharge your willpower, take a few minutes to look at the following list of values:

Friends	Helping others	Health	Fun and excitement
Influence	Personal growth	Freedom	Neatness/tidiness
Creativity	Respect	Children	Physical appearance
Travel	Family	Wealth	Sporting success
Spiritual growth	Adventure	Love	Kindness

Put the numbers 1 to 20 down the side of a sheet of paper and then copy out the list of values into a ranked order. So number 1 will be your most important value and number 20 the least important to you.

Trust your intuition. You'll almost immediately have an idea of what's truly important and what's not. Don't obsess about the precise order of the values in the bottom half of your list – we won't be considering them again. What's more crucial is to get a good sense of what your top three or four values might be. You only need to do this inaugural step once.

Once you've done that, spend six minutes – the length of time the participants spent – writing about your most important value. Write a short essay about *why* you pursue that value. Why is it so important to you? In the course of the exercise, you may write a little on what you're doing or have done to work on the value. But researchers have found that focusing on *why* a value is important offers the biggest boost to your willpower.

So there we have it. Six minutes writing about your value – that's all there is to it.

As you can imagine, though, it may be difficult to keep writing about your single most treasured value without simply copying out what you wrote the last time if you wish to deploy this nifty technique again and again. So I suggest that on the next occasion you need to boost your willpower, write about your second most important value. On a third occasion, write about your third most important value. By writing about your top three values on different occasions, you should hopefully be able to keep the exercise fresh.

We no longer need to wish we had more willpower. By writing about an important value we can help ourselves to withstand more discomfort and persist longer with troublesome tasks.

One of my clients, called Henri, swears by the technique. A quiet, unassuming French-born manager in his late twenties, he works in the go-getting environment of an investment firm. When we first met, he explained that most of his colleagues are brash, outgoing alpha-male types who are more than happy to be the centre of attention. They throw bawdy jokes and innu-endoes around, tease each other mercilessly, and compete to see who can drink the most on their frequent nights out in some of London's most exclusive pubs and bars.

Henri enlisted my support because he was worried that his quieter nature and reluctance to join in was holding him back career-wise. He wanted more responsibility and the larger salary that went with it, but he suspected that his bosses were promoting people they *liked* rather than those who were necessarily the best at the job. Given that he didn't socialise much with his colleagues, he was concerned that his bosses didn't know him well enough to like him.

I worked with Henri to devise a plan to build stronger relationships with both his colleagues and bosses. Part of it involved inviting individual colleagues and senior managers out for lunches and coffees to raise his profile and showcase his personality in a way that was comfortable for him. But another part necessitated going out more to team social events – there was simply no getting away from the fact that he needed to show that he was a team player.

It remains an ongoing battle. Henri has to fight against his nature, his innate tendency to shy away from boisterous group events. He works hard at telling entertaining stories about himself so that he comes across as lively, interesting and one of the gang. He finds it draining but says that writing about his values is his favourite manoeuvre for keeping his spirits and motivation high.

At least once a week, he writes about his relationship with his wife, his relationship with his parents and siblings, the football coaching he does with a youth team, or something else that he cherishes deeply. He has written about some of these topics more than once, but each time he starts afresh and writes about what he's valuing then and there rather than looking back at what he wrote the previous time. And he believes it's giving him the focus and mental fortitude he needs to come out of his shell a little more.

ONWARDS AND UPWARDS

➧ Remember that willpower is a finite resource. Use it up and you may find yourself struggling to resist temptations when you're feeling tired, hungry, irritable or simply lazy. Bear in mind that having to restrain yourself from shrieking at an incompetent colleague, for example, may make you less able to resist having a cigarette or unhealthy snack later on. So aim to avoid getting into stressful situations in the first place.

➧ If you can, remove temptations from your environment to preserve the willpower you have for when you really need it. Organise your work station, kitchen, bedroom or whichever parts of your life are relevant to make it easy for you to stick to your goals.

➧ Hone your willpower by performing small acts of self-control whenever you can, even if they might be unrelated to the changes you yearn for in your life. Training the mental muscle of your willpower for as little as two weeks has been proven to boost your chances of making the bigger changes you hope to make.

➧ For a quick boost of willpower, spend a few minutes writing about one of the most important values in your life and *why* you choose to pursue it. I'll give you a couple of variations on the basic exercise in The Motivation Toolkit at the back of the book too.

FOUR

SEEING SUCCESS

'I never see what has been done;
I only see what remains to be done.'
Buddha

Daniel is a partner at a mid-sized but growing law firm. He's the kind of person who stands out in a crowd. With eyebrows the thickness of caterpillars and a mane of dark hair that is the envy of many middle-aged men, the 47-year-old waves his hands around expansively as if he's directing traffic when talking. He has a louder than average voice and, if you were to meet him at a party, you'd probably hear his laughter from the other side of the room. He's not a quiet individual who shies away from the spotlight.

At least that's how Daniel appears to most people, because he sought support on becoming more confident at public speaking. By no means is he shy. He's more than happy to go up to strangers at parties or business events. But he hates, hates, *hates* giving presentations: his heart races, his throat goes dry, and his thoughts become preoccupied with what might go wrong. While he had managed to survive giving presentations – he wasn't awful at speaking in front of groups – he was aware that he wasn't as good as he should be for a senior manager either.

Over the course of several sessions, we worked out a couple of tactics for him to organise his thoughts more coherently so that his presentations hung together logically. But we also worked on his confidence. One of the techniques he found most useful for calming his nerves was visualisation. Sitting quietly at home or on the train on the way to work, he closed his eyes and pictured the presentation he needed to give. In his mind's eye, he would watch himself standing in front of his audience and running through the words of his actual presentation. And using his imagination gave him not only greater confidence but also helped him to deliver more winning speeches.

Hang on a second, though. Isn't daydreaming bad for us? You might remember at the very start of the introduction to this book (way back on page 4), I mentioned that daydreaming about a perfect future may actually have *harmful* effects. The study I brought up showed that students who daydreamed a lot about their future careers not only got fewer job offers but ultimately earned less than their more grounded peers. Indeed, more than one group of researchers have found that people who visualise glimpses of a desirable future may find themselves accomplishing *less* than those who don't.

Why then am I actively encouraging clients like Daniel to envision what the future may look like?

The truth is that not all forms of visualisation, imagery and fantasising are created equal. It turns out that some patterns of daydreaming and future-gazing may sap our energy and reduce our chances of making change happen in our lives. But certain other methods can help us to prepare for big events and make it less of a gamble that we can achieve the lives we want.

RECOGNISING THE DANGERS
OF WISHFUL THINKING

The Secret by Rhonda Byrne was a publishing phenomenon. The book sold millions of copies in dozens of languages worldwide. And the secret advocated within the book (as well as other New Age books of its ilk) seems to be that we can call upon some alleged magic of the universe to give us whatever we want – if only we wish for it hard enough.

We all do it sometimes: let our eyes defocus or even close and allow our thoughts to whisk us to a miraculous reality where all of our wishes have come true. When I was at school and sitting through tedious lessons in history or German – my least favourite subjects – I used to imagine that I was a superhero. Like Superman, I could fly and was astonishingly strong. I'd swoop down from the skies to defeat supervillains and the like.

When I was at university, I had a slightly more realistic fantasy: of having my own radio talk show and having people all over the country phoning in to seek my advice as a psychologist. I don't daydream so much these days, which is just as well because a solid body of evidence suggests that daydreaming and wishful thinking can have quite negative consequences.

In a rather intriguing study, for example, 25 obese women were asked about their fantasies prior to embarking on a year-long weight-loss programme. Some of the women worried about the future – their fantasies were filled with concerns that they wouldn't lose enough weight or that they might even put weight back on. Other women had upbeat fantasies of going to parties and having friends or even strangers marvel at how much slimmer and attractive they looked.

We tend to think of optimism as a good quality. We often find grumpy, downbeat people draining to be around. We may occasionally tell pessimistic friends not to worry and that things might turn out well in the end. And many of us who may have a more negative disposition often wish that we could be more positive. But when the researchers monitored the women's weight over the course of a year, they were stunned.

The more hopeful the women's fantasies were, the *less* weight they lost. The women who had negative images of what might occur in the future lost on average nearly 20 per cent of their body weight. However, the women with escapist visions of the future shed only half as much – less than 10 per cent.[18]

The study suggests that wallowing in positive daydreams may impair our chances of achieving our goals. More compelling evidence comes from a pair of experiments conducted in 2011 by New York University researcher Heather Kappes in conjunction with University of Hamburg psychologist Gabriele Oettingen. To give you an idea of these studies' importance, they were written up in one of the most prestigious behavioural science publications in the world, the *Journal of Experimental Social Psychology*.[19]

'Wallowing in positive daydreams may impair our chances of achieving our goals'

Before I tell you about the studies, may I ask you to take a very short quiz? Just three statements. Take a look at each adjective and please rate the extent to which you're feeling each of the following right now:

	1	2	3	4	5
	Very slightly or not at all	A little	Moderately	Quite a bit	Extremely
1. Excited					
2. Enthusiastic					
3. Active					

Total up your score to get a number between 3 and 15; I'll explain how this little quiz is relevant in a few moments.

In one experiment, Kappes and her associate recruited 50 volunteers for what they were told was a study on the effects of mental simulation on essay-writing performance. The research duo told the participants that they would be putting pen to paper to compose a short essay. To spur on the participants, they were told that the writer of the best essay would be awarded a $200 prize.

But first: the mental simulation. The participants were split into two groups. One group was asked to imagine that they had won the cash prize and that everything associated with the prize would turn out well. These participants were asked to jot down what they were thinking about.

One participant in this first group, for example, wrote:

> The best part about winning this $200 is that I don't have to be so stingy anymore. I can go out to dinner with friends and be social again. I have had to be so stringent with my spending recently and I have felt more distant from my friends BUT NOW we go to our favourite bar

*and get drunk on 4-dollar martinis. I am not worried
about how much anything costs because I have two
hundred in cash.*

A second group was told that winning the cash prize was *not* a certainty. These volunteers were told to imagine a somewhat gloomier future. For example, one of the participants in this control group wrote:

*I really need this prize. I do not need the money; instead I
need the feeling of joy that accompanies good luck. Now
I am not actually winning the two hundred dollar prize. I
wish that I had never known about the prize because now
I wish that I had something that I cannot have, whereas
before I just didn't have it.*

Immediately after jotting down their thoughts about either a positive or negative view of what might happen regarding the prize, both groups were asked to complete a short questionnaire to measure their energy levels. They noted their responses to the same three questions that I asked you a few moments ago.

Can you guess how the two groups reacted? Do you think that thinking about a wonderful future would rev up the participants more and that contemplating a negative future would drain them? Or the opposite: that thinking about a rosy future would sap their energy in comparison with thinking about how things might go wrong?

Analysing their data, the researchers found that the participants who imagined winning the prize – in other words a super-optimistic view of the future – actually felt *less* energetic.

Projecting themselves into a positive future seemed to have depleted their energy. They reported that they felt significantly less enthusiastic, active and excited.

The study shows that imagining idealised futures saps people's feelings of energy. So what, though? Feelings are just *feelings* – they're not the same as actions, right? Is that really so terribly noteworthy or thrilling? Big deal.

'Imagining idealised futures saps people's feelings of energy'

But in a second study, the researchers again asked two groups of volunteers to fantasise about either a positive or neutral future (rather than a negative future as they had in the first study). This time, instead of asking them how they felt after spending a few minutes imagining either a positive or neutral vision, the investigators measured the systolic blood pressure of the participants.

Systolic blood pressure is a good indicator of physiological activity. It rises when we exert ourselves physically, for example when we climb a flight of stairs or have to carry a couple of heavy grocery bags to the kitchen. But it also spikes when we're keyed up psychologically – such as when we're excited while watching a sports game on TV or nervous about a job interview. So when the participants who imagined an idyllic future experienced a drop in their blood pressure, the researchers knew that they had found undeniable evidence that positive daydreaming can rob us of not only our feelings of energy but also our physical vigour.

What seems to be occurring is that enjoying an overly positive reverie may create a sensation within us that is not unlike the afterglow of attaining a minor achievement. Imagining we've

achieved something gives us a fraction of the sense of satisfaction that comes from actually assembling some flat-packed
furniture successfully or knowing that you had a good workout
at the gym, cleaning the kitchen or returning home on a Friday
evening after a tiring week at work. We relax and let go. Both
our minds and bodies wind down, robbing us of the energy we
need to achieve what we're dreaming about.

So job-seekers sit back and put their feet up rather than send
out more application forms. Lonely singletons on the lookout
for love stay at home rather than go out to mingle. And all of
the many people who would like to transform their lives – wanting to lose weight, put more money into their savings, renovate
their homes, transform their attitudes and so on – decide to
stick with the status quo rather than put in the effort it takes to
make their goals come true.

The lesson is clear: if we want to make serious changes in
our lives, we might be wise to avoid wallowing too long in
escapist daydreams about what we *might* achieve. Because we
probably won't.

Of course, we all daydream occasionally. I caught myself
doing it recently. I was on a transatlantic flight to Toronto
and watched as some of the passengers waltzed up to the first-
class cabin where they would be pampered and indulged in the
finest luxuries available to anyone flying on a plane. For a few
whimsical moments, I wished I could fly first class too. But I
stopped myself. I cut short that rosy glimpse of what my life
could be like. Because if I want to achieve more, research clearly
tells me that I should focus on what I can *do* to move towards

my goals rather than the fantasy of what I might wish or hope to achieve.

OVER TO YOU

Studies strongly suggest that having daydreams – i.e. wishful fantasies and overly optimistic mental images of what we want – may trigger within us an illusory sense of achievement. It divorces us from reality and the steps we actually need to take. It saps our motivation and reduces the results we are likely to attain. However, please don't confuse that with having goals and targets.

A would-be entrepreneur who wants to set up a business should still set goals – perhaps writing down an ambition to have a dozen employees by the end of the year or to have earned a specific amount of money. An individual can still decide on a New Year's resolution to shed so much weight by a particular date. Someone who wants to be less lonely can still set a target of phoning and emailing say two or three friends every week.

So let me reiterate: the research only says that we shouldn't dwell on *excessively hopeful fantasies* – the mental pictures and the feel-good emotions that might go with them – about what we want to achieve. It's that wishful thinking and the wallowing in overly detailed mental movies of how we'd like our lives to turn out that we should minimise. In making change happen, we would all still benefit from having realistic goals and working out the implementation intentions that will help us to achieve them.

REHEARSING WHAT'S RIGHT

But visualisation clearly helps some people, including Serbian tennis star and world number-one ranked player Novak Djokovic. Cast your mind back just a few years: 2011 was a particularly amazing year and a turning point for the six-foot-two-inch tall athlete. The wiry Serbian outclassed Britain's Andy Murray to win the Australian Open and beat Spanish powerhouse Rafael Nadal to win both the US Open and the Wimbledon championship. Oh, and along the way he brushed aside a challenge from Roger Federer, himself one of the greatest players of all time.

Of course, reaching the pinnacle of success in any sport takes a combination of dedication, expert coaching, balanced nutrition, strenuous gym training sessions, the right genetics and lots and lots of hard work. But at least part of Djokovic's preparations are psychological: he carries out pre-match visualisation sessions to rehearse how he'd like to play.

Sitting quietly in the changing room before a game, he sees himself delivering hard-hitting serves: throwing the tennis ball directly above him before bringing his racquet round in a devastatingly powerful arc to smack the ball across the net into his opponent's court. He imagines himself swinging his arms round to punch the ball across the court beyond his opponent's reach. For several minutes, he imagines himself delivering overwhelmingly powerful backhands, forehands and volleys as well as deftly placed drop shots and slices.

His former coach Jelena Gencic spotted Djokovic's talent at just six years of age. She coached him for six years and, as part of his overall programme, encouraged him to develop his visualisation skills.

'I used classical music to teach him visualisation,' she recalled. 'We would listen to a composition and afterwards I would ask him what he heard and what he felt. One time after listening to Tchaikovsky's 1812 Overture, he said to me, "My heart feels blissful. And my skin is like the flesh of a goose." Can you imagine a seven-year-old boy feeling and saying such things?'[20]

Of course, Djokovic isn't the only sports star to believe in the power of visualisation. Typing the words 'sport' and 'visualisation' into Google brings up dozens of news articles in which both athletes and their coaches pay testimony to its benefits. In sports as diverse as archery, basketball, swimming, Australian football, gymnastics and golf, top athletes seem to be spending a significant amount of their time playing out carefully crafted mental movies in which they are the stars.

Could they *all* be wrong?

Playing detective in an attempt to answer precisely this question, a team of experts led by neuroscientist Carl-Johan Olsson from Umeå University in Sweden recruited a squad of 20 high jumpers – all of them elite competitors at a national level – to take part in a study on the effects of visualisation on athletic performance.

You may have seen high jumpers using a manoeuvre called the Fosbury Flop, which involves running towards the bar at a sharp angle and throwing themselves backwards over the bar with an arched back. Amazingly, the world record is a jump of 2.45

metres, which is the equivalent of jumping over someone six feet tall – and clearing them by an additional two feet!

The scientists began by recording videos of the athletes' high-jumping ability as if they were in an actual competition. Analysing the footage, the scientists calculated not only the height that the participants managed to clear but also bar clearance, which is a technical measure of the extent to which the athletes arch their backs by pulling their toes towards their heads in order to leap over the bar more efficiently.

Next, the scientists divided the athletes into two randomly chosen groups. The first, experimental group met with the researchers twice weekly for six weeks to engage in visualisation training. The participants were given the following instructions:

> Imagine that you are running towards the bar at a calm pace. At the curve, you are leaning slightly inwards towards the bar. On the last two steps, the legs run past the body and you lean slightly backwards. In the take-off, you plant the whole foot, you feel that the knee is straight, and you lean away from the bar. The lead leg bends and is parallel to the bar; the arms help you up. The take-off foot leaves the ground; you rotate so that your back is against the bar. You pull your heels towards your head so your back bends. You push your hips up and lean your head back and pull your legs over the bar. You land on the pit and you make the jump.

Not all of that quite makes sense to me, but then I'm not a high jumper. And I suspect that the English version lost something in translation from the original Swedish!

Anyway, the athletes were told to imagine the scene as directed. Some of the athletes imagined it with their eyes closed; others did so with their eyes open.

The second group acted as a control group. To ensure that any improvement in the experimental group was not just due to spending more time with the scientists, the athletes in the control group were brought in twice a week for six weeks too. But they were asked to spend the same length of time each session tapping their fingers. Yes, you read that correctly. A task completely unrelated to visualisation.

Finally, after six weeks, the scientists again set up a mock competition for the athletes. So did the athletes who had engaged in mental imagery exercises jump any higher?

No. Not at all. But that didn't surprise the scientists. After all, these were experienced athletes used to pushing themselves to their physical limits. So the scientists didn't expect that a few minutes of imagery over only six weeks would lift the athletes higher into the air.

But the group who learned the visualisation exercises did notch up a significant improvement in bar clearance – the technical measure of the degree to which the athletes bent their backs. Explaining the result, the scientists argued that bar clearance is the most cognitively complex aspect of the sport. To gain good bar clearance, high jumpers have to rotate their bodies in the air to face away from the bar and push their hips up, arching their spines to soar over the bar. While jump height is determined more by an athlete's physical strength and power, bar clearance requires a more intricate set of mental computations.[21]

Other behavioural scientists have come to much the same conclusion too. Imagery doesn't improve the aspects of performance that are based mainly on our physical characteristics – we wouldn't expect speed, strength or power to be affected. However, it may most benefit the more complex aspects of both sports and other activities that require skill or finesse.

So we wouldn't expect to lift heavier weights in the gym simply through visualisation. Nor would we anticipate being able to run any faster or to hit a tennis ball any harder. But we might expect that mental imagery training could help us in tasks requiring skill, such as aiming a tennis ball into an opponent's forecourt or hitting a golf ball more accurately. It might help when timing and technique matter – for example, a gymnast somersaulting over a pommel horse or an ice figure skater wanting to land a triple axel.

Of more interest for the rest of us who aren't top-flight athletes, visualisation may help us to perform better in all sorts of situations. It may help us when solving problems, giving speeches in public and negotiating with customers. It may help when we need to sell ourselves at interview, assert ourselves with loved ones or navigate the social etiquette of a first date.

FOCUSING ON MEANS VERSUS ENDS

So far we've established that some studies suggest that visualisation may reduce motivation and achievement; others show that it may improve confidence and performance, especially on the sports field. How can we resolve the apparent conflict?

The definitive study on how visualisation might benefit us or backfire was conducted by Lien Pham and Shelley Taylor, a pair of enquiring researchers at the University of California, Los Angeles (UCLA). The investigators hypothesised that people might visualise in broadly two different ways: they can either focus on the *outcomes* they desire or the *processes* they would follow to achieve their goals.

To test their theories, the investigators recruited nearly 100 undergraduate psychology students for a week-long study looking at the effects of different forms of mental imagery on exam performance. As with most well-run psychological studies, they randomly divided the students into several groups. One group was told to visualise themselves getting high scores on an upcoming exam. The students in the so-called 'outcomes' group read the following paragraph:

> In this exercise, you will be asked to visualise yourself
> getting a high grade on your Psychology midterm and
> imagine how you would feel. It is very important that
> you see yourself actually getting a high grade on the
> Psychology midterm and have that picture in your mind.

A second, so-called 'process' group was given instructions to focus on the practice of studying:

> In this exercise, you will be asked to visualise yourself
> studying for the midterm in such a way that would lead
> you to obtain a high grade. As of today and for the
> remaining days before the midterm, imagine how you
> would study to get a high grade on your Psychology

midterm. It is very important that you see yourself actually
studying and have that picture in your mind.

A third group was given no guidance on visualisation. These participants formed a control group to see how they would perform in their exams with no added psychological help or hindrance.

A week later, all of the students took their midterm exams, which were marked by professors who had no knowledge of the visualisation instructions that the students may or may not have been given.

Which form of visualisation – if any – resulted in the best exam results?

The students in the control condition who hadn't been taught how to visualise at all on average scored 77.68 per cent in their exams. In comparison, the students in the outcomes group who had focused on a positive result (i.e. gaining a high grade) scored only 72.57 per cent. It's not a huge difference but a momentous one nonetheless. A few minutes of envisioning a happy conclusion had resulted in a *worse* performance.

On the other hand, the process group students who had focused on the rituals and routines of studying itself scored higher than the control group with scores of 80.60 per cent. Again, not a massive difference but it suggests that taking a few minutes simply to *imagine* the act of studying had helped to boost their scores.

We can assume that students want to get the best possible results, right? So it suggests that visualisation – or at least mentally picturing the process of studying itself – may be a valuable tool for anyone wanting to improve their grades.

'Process imagery (i.e. focusing on the *means* of achieving what we want) may boost our performance'

More importantly for us, though, Pham and Taylor's study helps us to wade through the muddle of apparently mixed results with regards to visualisation. The main difference in whether visualisation may help or hinder us seems to come down to the types of images that we allow to unfold in our private mental movies. While imagining outcomes such as how we'd feel if we were to get an A grade seems to diminish our drive and ability to achieve our goals, imagining actual processes – poring over textbooks, memorising facts and going through sample questions – seems to improve our chances. Or, to use more specialist parlance, while process imagery (i.e. focusing on the *means* of achieving what we want) may boost our performance, it seems that outcome imagery (i.e. focusing on the *ends* we want) may do the opposite.[22]

Returning to tennis star Novak Djokovic for a moment, we can see what that might mean in practice. If he were to focus on possible outcomes, they might involve seeing himself receiving a trophy and holding it aloft while soaking up the crowd's adulation as the cameras flash all around him in an arena. Or he might picture himself spending his prize money and going off to buy a new house, a speedboat or whatever else he might desire. But no. Instead, Djokovic focuses on his serves, his volleys, his forehands and backhands and slices and drop shots. He imagines himself sprinting after the ball time after time, and all of the other steps that he must take in order to achieve his goal.

Suppose that a young man wants to overcome his shyness to date more and perhaps find someone special to share his life with him. A mental movie of the outcome might revolve around him living in a big house with a wife and family. He might see himself playing in the garden with his kids – one's a boy and the other is a girl – while his wife, the mother of his children, sits and watches the fun. On the other hand, visualising the process of dating might throw the spotlight on what he needs to do to actually meet more women: summoning up the courage to ask his pretty colleague out on a date, inputting his credit card details to join a dating website, or perhaps polishing his shoes and ironing a shirt to get ready to go on a date.

'Visualising *processes* can strengthen our resolve and boost our chances of successfully taking the steps we need to accomplish our goals'

Or let's imagine that a woman who runs a graphic design business wants to improve her business networking skills. If she visualises the outcome that she's hoping to achieve, she might bring to mind images of how successful her business has become, the plush offices she has moved her business into, and the gleaming industry awards sitting on her desk. But visualising the process would focus on more practical steps such as attending more conferences and seminars, introducing herself to fresh faces, and exchanging both conversation and business cards with the people she meets.

Outcome imagery is a form of daydreaming, escapism or wishful thinking. It focuses on what it might look and feel like to have crossed the finish line and achieved our goals. It projects us into a wonderful future when we've got what we wanted and are experiencing the benefits.

By contrast, process imagery is more focused on mental rehearsal of the behaviours we want to undertake. It directs our attention to the steps we might take in order to reach the desired outcome; it focuses on the challenges we must overcome, the effort we must invest and the day-to-day reality of working towards our goals.

In comparing the effects of the two types of mental movie-making, the research is clear. Visualising *outcomes* allows us to feel good immediately, but in doing so we experience a false sense of accomplishment that robs us of the drive, the hunger, we need to take action. Visualising *processes*, on the other hand, can strengthen our resolve and boost our chances of successfully taking the steps we need to accomplish our goals.

CREATING MOTIVATING MENTAL MOVIES

So how exactly do we go about visualising scenes that will help us to achieve our goals?

For the answer, we turn to the work of Bärbel Knäuper, a psychologist and an authority in the promotion of healthy eating at McGill University in Montreal. In 2011, she and a group of colleagues decided to look at the interplay between both implementation intentions and visualisation in volunteers who all wanted to improve their diets by eating more fruit every day.

In Chapter Two: Setting Effective Goals, you may remember that I talked at length about how writing out a set of implementation intentions can improve our chances of turning our goals into reality. For example, rather than having a vague intention to 'exercise more', a set of more specific implementation intentions might include promises to 'run in the park on Saturday morning for 30 minutes after I've made breakfast for the kids' and 'go for a swim on Monday evenings after work'.

Knäuper and her colleagues wanted to know whether implementation intentions and visualisation together would produce better results than either alone. Or might the two interact in some unexpected way and perhaps cancel each other out?

You know the drill by now: participants were recruited and then randomly assigned to different conditions, with each group of participants receiving slightly different instructions. The first group was directed to write out a set of standard implementation intentions.

A second group was taught how to deploy mental imagery to picture themselves eating more fruit. Part of their instructions read as follows:

> We would like you to do a mental imagery exercise in order to improve your chances of achieving the goal. Please mentally imagine yourself consuming extra portions of fruit each day for the next seven days. Make sure to use all of your senses in your mental imagery of

this intention: notice how the fruits or fruit juices look, feel, taste, and smell. Notice how it sounds when you bite into them or when you drink them. Really take a moment to close your eyes and imagine this intention.

A third group was taught both techniques – to create a set of implementation intentions *and* to use visualisation. A fourth, control group were taught no further skills to see how much fruit participants would eat without any additional training.

Monitoring the dietary habits of the participants, the researchers noticed that both implementation intentions and mental imagery were equally effective at bumping up the amount of fruit that the participants ate when compared with the control group. However, the largest increase in fruit intake came from the group that learnt *both* techniques.[23]

'Visualisation has an additive effect over and above that of scribbling out implementation intentions'

The implication: visualisation has an additive effect over and above that of scribbling out implementation intentions. Use the two together and you get the biggest bang for your buck.

OVER TO YOU

The key to successful visualisation is to use it *after* you have created your set of implementation intentions. Then you can spend a few moments picturing each of your individual implementation intentions.

Someone wanting to work more productively in order to get a promotion at work might have an implementation intention to 'spend Saturday mornings catching up on paperwork'. He could help to lock that picture into his mind by envisioning himself sat in his study typing away on his computer and his favourite classical music tinkling away in the background.

Someone else who wants to control her temper may have decided that her most important implementation intention is to 'stop talking if I'm feeling angry and just breathe'. She might benefit from closing her eyes and imagining herself having a conversation with her husband that's on the verge of escalating into a quarrel but interrupting herself to breathe deeply for a few seconds.

Using the instructions given by Bärbel Knäuper and her colleagues to the participants who combined both implementation intentions with visualisation, here's a set of instructions you could use to formulate your own mental images:

Research has shown that you are even more likely to carry out your implementation intention action plan if you mentally visualise each of your actions in turn. For each of your actions, take a few moments to create a mental image of where (e.g. at home, the office, the gym, a restaurant and so on) and when (e.g. a particular time of day or day of the week) you might perform each action. Notice how your environment looks: pick out the details that help to bring your mental image to life. See yourself in the picture as if you were looking at the scene as an observer and see yourself performing the action (e.g. exercising, cooking a healthy meal, asserting yourself with a colleague, asking someone out on a date, etc.).

Notice how the scene looks. Allow yourself to feel the sensations and emotions you might feel. Bring taste and smell into the scene if it's appropriate too. The more vivid and detailed your mental movie, the better your chances of taking action successfully.[24]

A friend – a single mother in her late thirties with two teenage sons – is trying to be more organised. Niamh (pronounced 'Neeve') admits that her life is more than a little chaotic. She has wanted to get more organised for years, not only with the physical clutter at home, but also with her finances and even her social life. After spending every weekday at work and then cooking dinner for her boys every evening, she usually ends with her feet up watching TV rather than doing the household chores that, in an ideal world, she'd like to get done.

To boost her motivation, I have at times suggested that she could do a spot of visualisation. On the train on the way home from work, for example, she could close her eyes and picture herself doing the tasks she needs to do: sitting at the kitchen table with her laptop and the bills and other correspondence she needs to deal with; chivvying her sons, Brendan and Dylan, to tidy their rooms; perhaps cleaning the bathroom, tidying the lounge or even removing clutter from her own wardrobe.

Suppose that you're on a fitness drive and want to give yourself the best shot at actually going to the gym or your Zumba class when you finish work on a given day. It might be worth seeing yourself – maybe during your lunch hour or even when you have an idle moment between tasks during the day – picking up your sports bag, sauntering along to your gym and saying 'hello' to the receptionist when you arrive.

Or say you made a New Year's resolution to read more books and watch less television. To strengthen your resolve, close your eyes occasionally for a few seconds and imagine yourself curled up on your couch, a steaming cup of your favourite drink in hand, turning the pages of your chosen book. Mental simulation can be an incredibly effective sleight of mind – one that's literally only limited by the power of your imagination.

ONWARDS AND UPWARDS

➡ In Chapter One: Getting Ready for Change, I discussed evidence that people who spend a little time thinking about the benefits of change are more likely to motivate themselves into taking action to achieve change. However, avoid spending too much time projecting yourself into an idealised future of what it might feel like to have achieved your goal. It's the difference between doing 'some' visioning versus 'too much'. Spending overly long on the outcomes you wish to accomplish may actually reduce your motivation and worsen your chances of changing.

➡ Instead, focus on the steps you'll take to achieve your goals. Even better, use visualisation *after* you've worked out your implementation intentions so you can focus on seeing yourself performing each of them in detail.

➡ Engage as many of your senses as you can when visualising the steps you wish to take. Use your imagination to summon up relevant sights, colours, smells and even tastes if it's appropriate.

➡ Remember above all to focus on the steps (the process) that will allow you to carve out the life you want rather than the results (the outcome). When it comes to actually turning your goals into reality, process = good; outcome = bad.

FIVE

DEVELOPING GREATER EMOTIONAL RESILIENCE

'Failure is simply the opportunity to begin again,
this time more intelligently.'
Henry Ford

Hannah has been a somewhat bashful friend of mine since we were both teenagers. She had a handful of relationships that lasted several years apiece in her twenties. But in her early thirties, she found herself single. After quite a few years of wanting to be in a fulfilling relationship, she made up her mind that it was time to take charge. Rather than waiting for the fates to present her with the right man, she signed up to one of the more respectable Internet dating websites.

With her long, ink-black hair, shy smile and enviable figure, Hannah attracted plenty of attention from admirers. But she was often disappointed. Some of the men she met had patently lied about themselves. One claimed on his dating profile to have been educated to degree level, but confessed over dinner he had left school without any qualifications. More than a few of her potential suitors put themselves into the 35–44 age range on their dating profiles but turned out to be in the 45–54 age range. And others used photos of themselves from long ago – from before they put on lots of weight or when they still had a full head of hair.

After each disappointment, she toyed with giving up. What was the point in going on?

And then there were the rejections, which were the most hurtful. On a handful of occasions, she found herself dating a man for perhaps several months and warming to him only for the budding relationship to come to an end. One man inexplicably cut off all communications with her and refused to take her calls. A few told her that they didn't think there was enough chemistry – they didn't like her enough – to continue seeing her. Another admitted that he was married and simply looking for an extramarital fling.

Her emotional life turned into a rollercoaster. One week she was ecstatic; the next she could be frustrated or downright despondent.

There's a happy ending to Hannah's journey, though. Fast-forward to the present and she is married to Paul. They've been together for nearly two years and, shortly after her fortieth birthday, she announced that they were expecting their first child together.

Achieving the changes we want in life can be tough. Like Hannah, we are all likely to experience mishaps and frustration, rejection and failure along the way. It's the rare person who sets out to make meaningful transformations in life and doesn't waver or stumble at least occasionally.

Say someone we know makes a grand change in her life, such as taking a job in a foreign country. Of course, she will have days when she misses her friends and family, when she longs for the familiar sights and sounds of home. When she feels low, she may be less productive at work and less willing to invest effort in making new friends. Without lifting herself from her emotional funk, she could sabotage her own chances of making the transition successfully.

The same applies to all of us when we make even small tweaks in our lives. Suppose we're trying to exercise regularly, think more positively or stop biting our nails. There will be days when we fall back into long-standing habits. We all have bad days when we succumb to temptation. And when we feel down, we may be tempted to give up on the whole notion of change. Learning to manage our emotions in the wake of relapses and rejections, missteps and blunders is an essential part of achieving change.

For some people, managing their emotions can be a major goal in its own right. I know many people who would like to overcome anxiety or escape from prolonged periods of despondency. A few wish they could control their tempers. Others want to feel more positive and confident from one day to the next.

> **'Learning to manage our emotions in the wake of relapses and rejections, missteps and blunders is an essential part of achieving change'**

So this chapter tackles the skill of handling our emotions – either as an aid to change or as an aim of change in its own right. For decades now, psychologists have been hoarding evidence about the techniques that both do and don't work when it comes to quelling our sometimes tumultuous emotions. But first, have you ever wondered: why do we have emotions at all?

UNDERSTANDING THE PURPOSE OF NEGATIVE EMOTIONS

As a psychologist, I often get invited to give keynote speeches at company conferences. Occasionally I get to listen to the talks of other presenters too. I remember listening to one particular motivational speaker – a frenetically energetic individual who shall remain nameless, as I'm about to criticise him – claim that we should be able to see the positives in *any* predicament, no matter how bad.

The hyperbolic guru explained that he was once in a car crash. He broke both of his hips and both legs, spending months in a wheelchair and another year in physical therapy. But he claimed that, rather than allowing himself to feel at all unhappy or depressed, he had used the time to think about his work and to record a series of audio books on motivation and coping with adversity. His conclusion was that we should all likewise be able to shut off all negative emotions simply by force of will.

Can we all really do that? *Should* we even aspire to do that?

Let's think about his claim for a moment: that we should never feel gloomy or despondent *no matter what's happening to us*. So if a loved one gets diagnosed with cancer, we should be able to smile and feel happy? Or if we get fired from our job and our home gets repossessed, we should look at how it's an opportunity to rejoice or even relax?

No. Clearly not. I disagreed totally, completely and fundamentally with his argument.

When things go awry, it would be inappropriate to try to feel only joy and delight. It would be inhuman *not* to experience negative emotions.

But our emotions don't just make us human. They serve a vital purpose too.

In a now classic and influential paper summarising decades of research on the topic, psychologists Charles Carver and Michael Scheier suggested that our emotions form an in-built system for monitoring the rate at which we're achieving our goals.[25] The central idea is that we experience positive emotions such as happiness and excitement when we're making good or better-than-expected progress towards our goals. When we experience positive emotions, we feel good, which reinforces the fact that we should continue to do more of what we're already doing.

> 'While we need *healthy* negative emotions, we must be watchful that we don't let *unhealthy* negative emotions beat us down'

But we experience negative emotions – unhappiness, frustration, regret, for example – when we're making less progress than we crave. When that happens, our feelings are designed to make us consider our options, put in more effort or change tactics and do things differently.

The point is that negative emotions have a purpose. They provide us with useful information in signalling to our brains that we should be taking some form of appropriate action. No one is – or *should* be – impervious to feeling bad. An inability to experience unpleasant emotions would rob us of useful feedback – it's a survival mechanism that tells us when we're in a genuinely threatening situation. Or we might forge on regardless and never learn when we need to behave differently.

Having said that, though, it's unhelpful when we allow our emotional upheaval to overwhelm us or when we wallow in unhappiness for too long. Negative emotions are a necessary and useful part of being human – it's only when we allow them to dominate our lives that it isn't healthy. And so we come to a headline-grabbing distinction: while we need to experience *healthy* negative emotions, we must be watchful that we don't let *unhealthy* negative emotions beat us down.[26]

APPRECIATING OUR CAPACITY FOR DISAPPOINTMENT, FEAR, ANGER AND GUILT

To illustrate the distinction between healthy and unhealthy negative emotions, allow me to talk you through a handful of hypothetical scenarios. Bear with me and we'll explore why even the harshest feelings may have a purpose.

To begin with, imagine that you're on the lookout for a new job. You read about a fantastic job, apply for it and get invited to interview. You get on well with your would-be colleagues at interview and you genuinely like the sound of the work and the company. Unfortunately, you get one of those 'we enjoyed meeting you, but . . .' letters – you don't get the job. Anyone would feel disappointed; no one is suggesting that you should clap your hands with glee and celebrate.

The disappointment has a function. It may make you ask yourself: was there anything you did or said that might not have gone down well? More importantly, if you did trip up, how might you avoid the same gaffe in your next interview?

Once the negative emotion has served its purpose, though, you would need to pick yourself back up and apply for the next job and perhaps the one after that. The danger is in letting that disappointment (a healthy negative emotion) turn into a depression (an unhealthy negative emotion) so deep and prolonged that you give up your job search entirely. That way, you definitely won't get your dream job.

Not all negative emotions are created equal. Some inkling of an unpleasant feeling may be healthy and helpful; but too much of it may be unhealthy and thwart us from achieving our goals.

For example, consider how you might feel if your boss were to ask you to give a presentation to the entire department. Your boss hints that your performance could lead to fresh responsibilities, a promotion and even a pay rise if it goes well. Now if you're not a practised public speaker, you would be right to feel concerned. A healthy negative emotion of apprehension – a touch of fear – would motivate you to prepare your speech well in advance, rehearse it a couple of times and make sure you deliver a brilliant presentation.

But what happens should you let your apprehension overwhelm you? It turns into the unhealthy negative emotion of outright anxiety. Frazzled with panic, you may worry so much that you might try to get out of giving the presentation. Or you let your concerns preoccupy you so much that you deliver a rambling, incoherent presentation. Either way, you don't rise to meet the challenge and lose out.

What about other emotions? Does anger, for example, have a purpose?

Well, let's suppose that a friend of yours says she desperately needs to borrow some money because she has a lot of bills to pay this month and won't have enough money to feed herself properly until her next pay cheque. She's really worried that she will have to go hungry. Naturally, you lend her the money.

But imagine that you later discover that she has gone and spent the money on a new dress for an upcoming party and, as a result, has survived on nothing more than breakfast cereal for a week. That's not right, is it? You'd be right to feel annoyed – as much for her sake as anything else.

A healthy sense of frustration and displeasure may encourage you to confront her and get her to alter her ways. If she doesn't watch her budget more carefully, she might get into serious trouble. If you didn't feel wound up, she might never learn. But by the same token, if you let that annoyance turn into outright rage (an unhealthy negative emotion), you could end up having a screaming match about all sorts of other grievances that you have each been saving up. And that would benefit no one.

Or suppose that you're on a diet. You've been doing well for a couple of months now. But one evening you blow it by having a massive dinner and *two* helpings of dessert. The following morning, you realise you're not going to hit your weight-loss goals at your next monthly weight-loss club weigh-in. Of course, you might feel regretful or guilty. Regret and guilt are unpleasant feelings that we want to avoid, so by experiencing them on this occasion, your mind is attempting to warn you off from having to experience them again in the near future. It's similar to feeling pain after touching a scalding hot saucepan – it's your mind's way of making you less likely to touch a fiery object ever again. Regret and guilt may motivate you to behave differently next time, so they are healthy negative emotions.

The important thing is not to feel shame, the notion that you're a worthless human being. When you feel regret or guilt, you feel at fault for something you did or said *on one occasion* – you admit that it was a mistake and you try to move on. But people who feel shame often fall into the trap of believing that they are stupid, useless, irredeemable people and that there's nothing good about themselves at all – that they are at fault *all of the time*. If you feel ashamed of yourself, you implicitly label yourself a bad person.

'It's only when we allow negative emotions to drown us that they become unhealthy'

And once you believe that you're bad to the core, what's the point in trying to change? While regret and guilt may push you to avoid giving into temptation in the future, shame could cause you to give up and stop trying entirely.

To sum up, we have negative emotions for a reason. They are part of our in-built alarm system, alerting us to obstacles, problems and threats. Experiencing *some* level of negative emotions is entirely healthy. It would be unnatural not to feel sadness at the loss of a loved one, annoyance when others treat us unfairly, or a touch of nerves when we're asked to take on fresh challenges.

It's only when we allow negative emotions to drown us that they become unhealthy. So while we should embrace a healthy level of negative emotion, psychologists increasingly recommend that we should guard against letting those unpleasant feelings spiral into unhealthy negative emotions that prevent us from reaching our goals.[27]

Shall we discuss a handful of practical techniques for doing precisely that?

ARTICULATING ANXIETIES

To introduce the first technique that allows us to keep our emotions in check, let me tell you about something that happened to a colleague of mine. A couple of years ago, Ethan – a fellow psychologist – received a shock when he and his family returned home from a two-week holiday abroad. Opening the front door to the house, they discovered a scene of mayhem: cupboards had been emptied and drawers pulled out of dressers, their contents thrown to the floor. Vases had been smashed and bookcases upended. Even the refrigerator and freezer had been flung open so there was spoiling food strewn all over the kitchen. Criminals had broken in and ransacked the house.

Both Ethan and his wife are pragmatic, sensible individuals, so they alerted the police about the break-in, reported it to their insurers and got on with the business of sorting out their home. Their 13-year-old son was more intrigued by the whole affair than annoyed or upset by the upheaval in his home.

Sadly, the youngest member of the family, Sophie, found the experience understandably harrowing. A sensitive eight-year-old, she loved dressing up as a mermaid and playing with her outsized cuddly green frog toy that she'd named Albert but affectionately called Alboo. On her first night home, she insisted on sleeping with her parents and carried on sleeping with them for several weeks.

When she was eventually persuaded to return to her own bed, she was anxious and unhappy and often woke in the night suffering from bad dreams. So her parents bought her a set of Guatemalan worry dolls. Each of the dolls is a stick of wood about the length of an adult's thumb and wrapped in little yarn clothes with thread stitching for eyes and loose strands of yarn for hair.

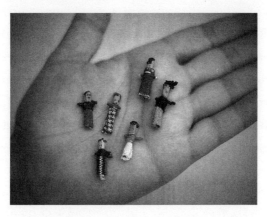

In Guatemala, parents give these rudimentary dolls to their children and say, 'If you have something that you're worried about, share each of your concerns with a different doll. Then tuck them under your pillow and while you're asleep the dolls will take your worries away.'

In suburban Britain, Ethan and his wife told Sophie that the dolls would carry her fears away so that she could slumber undisturbed. Little Sophie wasn't entirely convinced to begin with, but gave it a try; she whispered her secret fears to her dolls every evening before popping them into a tiny cloth pouch and slipping it beneath her pillow.

Miraculously, the dolls worked. Within weeks she was sleeping through the night again. And, while she was still not entirely convinced that burglars could not break into the house, her feelings of anxiety subsided to manageable levels.

Had the worry dolls come to life in the night and magically whisked her fears away? Probably not. So how did they help to reduce Sophie's distress?

In search of answers to such questions, we turn to the work of Matthew Lieberman, a highly decorated researcher at UCLA and the creator of a field of study called social cognitive neuroscience – the investigation of how thoughts and emotions are processed by different parts of the brain. His somewhat macabre research often centres on showing strangers some truly gruesome and repulsive photographs, and the study we will consider is no different.

In a 2011 experiment, he enlisted a group of volunteers to sit at a computer and told them that a series of photos would appear on screen. The participants' task was simply to report how they felt in response to each photo. Some of the photos were neutral in terms of the emotions that they aroused – for example, shots of people wearing neutral expressions or in everyday situations such as driving a car or buying groceries. However, some of the photos were extremely unpleasant to look at – ranging from images of a woman crying or a robbery in progress to photos of severe injuries and bodily mutilation.

I did consider asking for permission from the researchers to reproduce a couple of the photos here. But trust me, you don't want to see them. As expected, then, the volunteers who were shown such photos told the researchers that they felt 'very' upset by them.

However, Lieberman and his investigators then taught the volunteers a simple trick for insulating themselves from the distress of such photos. How?

The volunteers were simply asked to describe the scenes they saw. For example, to say out loud that the starving and perilously thin child in the photo was crying or that a corpse was being cut open to expose the internal organs within. All they had to do was put what they were seeing into words.

'The mere act of articulating what we are seeing or experiencing is enough to help us distance ourselves from the turmoil we feel'

And the practically effortless technique worked. The volunteers now felt much less distressed when they described the scenes they saw.[28]

Scientists call the technique 'affect labelling'. The mere act of articulating what we are seeing or experiencing is enough to help us distance ourselves from the turmoil we feel. It doesn't stop us from feeling bad entirely, but it may at least blunt the effects of our sometimes crazy emotions.

OVER TO YOU

The technique of 'affect labelling' allows us to dampen down the negative emotions we feel. And it's delightfully easy to use. We can do this simply by describing what's happening to us.

For example, say you get into an argument and you get really worked up. Rather than allowing the feelings of anger and worry to wash over you and drown you, try to describe the situation out loud – something like, 'I've had an argument with Patrick and because he said I was stupid and insensitive, I'm now feeling incredibly angry.'

Or suppose you're on your way to a big date, a job interview or a presentation to a group of senior colleagues at work. If you're panicking, take a few moments to sit quietly and describe the preparation you've done and what you hope to be doing – you can mutter it quietly to yourself or simply hear the words in your head if you might be overheard.

The very act of describing our circumstances seems to quieten the parts of our brain that are responsible for churning up our emotions. And this may help to take the edge off of what we're feeling.

Being more aware of our emotions may be especially important when we're trying to break bad habits and adopt better ones. For example, many people rely on bad habits – drinking more alcohol than they should, eating sugary snacks, biting their nails, venting at loved ones, smoking and so on – as ways to alleviate feelings of anxiety or frustration. Articulating how we're feeling by saying, 'I am feeling anxious because . . .' or 'I am feeling embarrassed because . . .' may reduce those emotions and help us to steer clear of those inappropriate ways of behaving.

I occasionally have the privilege of working with professional sports teams and athletes. Often, I run seminars about leadership and the behaviours that leaders use to inspire and motivate their teams. Sometimes, I help them to plan ahead for their careers once they have finished with the sport, as the physical toll on their bodies means that most can only compete for so many years. But because these guys (so far, all the athletes I've worked with have been men) are at the peak of their disciplines, they often work with other psychologists too.

A preternaturally gifted sportsman I'll call Craig passed on a technique that he had been taught. When he doesn't perform well in a game, rather that naming his emotions by saying, 'I am angry,' or 'I am frustrated,' he prefers to say, 'I am currently experiencing a feeling of anger, but it won't last forever,' or 'I am currently feeling frustrated, but it will pass.'

He explained, 'I am a human being. I am an adult. I am a father, a husband, and many things. But I am not anger, disappointment or any other feeling.'

He believed that saying, 'I am currently experiencing a feeling of . . . but it won't last forever,' rather than 'I am . . .' reminds him that any emotion he is feeling is likely to be only transitory, no matter how strong it might seem in the moment. He felt that doing so makes it easier for him to retain his emotional equilibrium when things aren't going well. Perhaps it works by creating an even greater separation between the rational part of his mind and his more primal emotions.

SEEING THINGS DIFFERENTLY

There may be even better ways to keep our emotions in check. Matthew Lieberman and his fellow scientists went one step further, by running another experiment and training more volunteers in a nifty technique that was an extension of affect labelling. This second group of participants was again told that they would see both neutral and intensely negative photographs. But when they saw the off-putting photos, they were urged to make up reasons that would allow the scenes to be perceived in a more positive manner.

So a volunteer seeing a photo of an obviously starving and unhappy child might have said, 'The picture was taken just before the child was rescued by aid workers and given food to eat.' A volunteer who was presented with a shot of a man in a hospital bed might have said, 'The patient has a strong consti-tution and is likely to recover.' Or a volunteer who looked at a scene of a woman being hit by a man might have concocted a story that 'the woman is about to reach for a phone to call the police and have him arrested'.

The technique is called 'reappraisal' – devising a reason or story that allows an ordeal to be assessed in a more optimistic way. When the researchers compared the results of affect labelling versus reappraisal, they found that participants who used reappraisal experienced an even greater damp-ening down of the negative emotions aroused by the photos.

'Reappraisal can help us to become the architects of our own emotions when times are tough'

The benefits of reappraisal aren't merely confined to the laboratory either. No, there wouldn't be much point in that, would there? A team of psychological inves-tigators from the University of Denver in Colorado recently conducted a survey of several hundred men and women who had gone through a stressful life event within the last three months – such as financial problems, health worries or difficulties at work. The researchers invited these people to complete a battery of psychological tests and found that the individuals who reported the greatest use of the reappraisal technique also had the highest levels of psychological well-being.[29]

In other words, the conscious use of reappraisal can help us to become the architects of our own emotions when times are tough. We can decide to take the sting out of vexing situations at will. Fancy giving it a go?

OVER TO YOU

Reappraisal is an even more potent version of affect labelling. Rather than merely describing a situation, it involves making up a reason or concocting a story that allows an ordeal to be seen in a more positive light.

That may sound artificial but the good news is that the manoeuvre helps to blunt the effects of negative emotions even when we ourselves don't believe the reasons or stories we're coming up with. The volunteers in Lieberman's study didn't have to *believe* that a starving child in a photo was about to be rescued or that a woman who was the victim of physical abuse would turn the tables on her assailant. It's the act of generating a reason or story that helps the more rational parts of our brains to take over. Whether we genuinely believe those reasons or stories doesn't matter. It's almost as if we can knowingly tell a lie to the more emotional branches of our own brains, but those parts go along with it anyway.

So if you're feeling agitated about an imminent job interview, you might tell yourself that it's an opportunity for you to assess whether you like the organisation rather than the other way around. If you're feeling angry and upset after a confrontation with a colleague, you might take a few moments to speculate that he's taking it out on you because he himself had a squabble with his wife that morning.

And remember that you don't have to *believe* the stories you tell yourself. The mere act of choosing to review your predicament and to cast it in a different light is in itself enough to liberate yourself a little from the negative emotions you may be feeling.

Just a few days ago, on a typically cold British winter's afternoon, I encouraged a friend to use the reappraisal technique when she was feeling glum. Miyuki warned me straight away when we met for lunch that she wasn't in the best of moods. She had spent the previous evening at a pub with some of her girl friends celebrating a mutual friend's birthday, but hadn't enjoyed the evening. She thought her friends were being cliquey – they weren't including her in the conversation. In the end, she feigned tiredness and left the get-together early.

I simply asked her, 'Might there be another explanation for what happened?'

She thought about it for a few seconds and said that her two closest friends had been sat at the other end of the table. She had been stuck with a few people she hadn't known quite so well. And the background music was so loud that she'd had difficulty hearing much.

With only a little more prompting on my part, Miyuki decided that maybe it had only been bad luck that she'd been left out of the conversation rather than artfulness on the part of her friends. Over the course of literally just a few minutes, her mood lifted and she was smiling again.

The next time you feel down about something – whether it's to do with your attempts to change your life, or indeed just about anything else – you

Ask, 'What might be another way of looking at this situation?'

might like to try it for yourself. You may even be able to help the people around you to shirk off their darker moods. Ask, 'What might be another way of looking at this situation?'

BOTTLING UP BAD FEELINGS

One tactic for managing negative emotions seems peculiarly British. Perhaps it's a remnant of public-school education from a bygone era, but British men in particular are most likely to be afflicted with the feeling that they should 'keep a stiff upper lip' – in other words, put on a smile or at least a stoic expression rather than reveal the pain or hurt they may actually be feeling.

The archetypal example would be of a British war hero – imagine an upper-class officer in the British army in a hackneyed Second World War film. He's been shot and is slowly, agonisingly bleeding to death. His comrades all know that he won't survive; the officer himself knows that he won't make it. But he still insists on putting on a brave face and telling people, 'Really, I'm fine. Don't worry about me.'

Of course, that's an extreme illustration, but even today, some people still prefer to hide or suppress their emotions. A close friend I was at school with – I'll call him Jeremy – is under an incredible amount of stress at work at the moment. The company he works for is struggling and has made round after round of job cuts. For over a year now, he's been working extraordinarily long hours in a bid to hold on to his job. When I ask him how he's doing, he describes the issues he's facing in an impersonal, matter-of-fact fashion. But I know the truth. Privately, his wife tells me that he seems beaten down and unhappy at home. He just refuses to let on how he's really feeling most of the time.

Obviously, Jeremy feels that walling off his feelings and pretend-ing he's okay works for him. But does it work for the rest of us?

One pair of researchers set out to test the effectiveness of suppression against reappraisal. We've already encountered the reappraisal technique, which involves looking at situations differently – forcing ourselves to make up alternative reasons and stories for the things that we may be seeing or feeling. Which would be the more powerful technique?

Again, I draw upon research done by esteemed behavioural scientists. Psychologists James Gross of Stanford University and Oliver John at the University of California, Berkeley, developed a test called the Emotion Regulation Questionnaire (ERQ), which measures the extent to which people use two popular tactics for handling the sometimes cruel effects of our emotions.

The first of the two tactics is reappraisal. So half of the ques-tionnaire tests how readily people reinterpret situations to help themselves to feel less bad. For example, they're asked to indicate the extent to which they agree or disagree with statements such as:

⇒ 'When I want to feel less negative emotion, I change the way I'm thinking about the situation.'

⇒ 'I control my emotions by changing the way I think about the situation I'm in.'

⇒ 'When I'm faced with a stressful situation, I make myself think about it in a way that helps me to stay calm.'

As I'm sure you can see, all three of those statements are about our ability to reappraise our circumstances or to see them in a different light. So that's our capacity for consciously and deliberately conjuring up a different set of reasons to explain how a situation may have come about.

The second of the two tactics was measured by a different set of statements. These statements included:

⇒ 'I control my emotions by not expressing them.'

⇒ 'I keep my emotions to myself.'

⇒ 'When I am feeling negative emotions, I make sure not to express them.'

This second set of questions clearly measures people's use of suppression, their tendency to hold in their emotions without showing them to the outside world. If you're upset, for example, that might mean trying to wear a neutral expression on your face. It might mean trying to control the tone of your voice to avoid letting on that you're feeling overwrought. When concerned friends ask how you are, you might say, 'I'm fine' and change the subject, or go a step further to claim, 'I'm feeling great, actually!'

Both reappraisal and suppression are popular strategies for managing negative emotions. But just because something is done by a lot of people, that doesn't make it appropriate and helpful. Indeed, when the researchers surveyed people who tended to use one tactic over the other, they found that the two have completely different effects on not only how we feel about ourselves but also how other people feel about us.

For a start, people who used reappraisal scored well on just about every aspect of psychological well-being. They reported being satisfied with their lives, being optimistic and having a high sense of self-esteem. In contrast, people who relied more on suppression reported a gloomier outlook – they suffered from more depressive symptoms, had lower self-esteem and were less optimistic.

Individuals who favoured reappraisal were likewise better at repairing their mood. In other words, re-construing a situation helped them to feel better – or at least to feel less bad – more quickly than those who tried to wall off their emotions and pretend that they felt all right. People who used suppression were often more successful at hiding their distress from the outside world, but as a result they tended to mull over the events that made them unhappy for much longer.

But it wasn't just that reappraisal or suppression affected the individuals who used those tactics. When the researchers persuaded friends to rate their friendships with people who were either reappraisers or suppressors, it turned out that the two tactics also had profound implications for the strength of those friendships. Individuals who used reappraisal to reformulate the meaning of situations were better liked by their friends than individuals who used suppression to stifle the emotions they felt. While friends found reappraisers to be warm and likeable people, the friends of suppressors tended to find them to be a little cool and detached.[30]

Our friends may be able to detect – consciously or subconsciously, we don't know – when we hold back what we're really feeling. They may wonder why we're trying to hide how we're feeling, why we're not being ourselves. That sense that we're trying to deceive them may cause them to doubt us. Why should they invest in a friendship with us if we don't trust them enough to be entirely honest with them?

In summary, the evidence suggests that suppression typically has dramatically less successful outcomes than reappraisal. Individuals who use suppression may think that burying their emotions and pretending that they're okay can help them to cope with adversity, but it seems that it may have precisely the opposite effect: it may make them feel more anxious, more depressed. Suppression may even put up a barrier that prevents our friends from knowing us as well – it may stop the people we cherish from returning the feelings we have for them.

> 'Suppression typically has dramatically less successful outcomes than reappraisal'

OVER TO YOU

The message is clear. Both studies that ask people how they feel *and* studies that directly monitor the brains of volunteers come to the same conclusions. Reappraisal helps us to negotiate stressful situations; it allows us to reinterpret challenging circumstances in ways that repair our mood as quickly as possible. Suppression, on the other hand, does the opposite of what we hope it might.

Are you someone who ever uses suppression as a tactic?

Let's have a look at some of the statements on the Emotion Regulation Questionnaire (ERQ) again. Do you find yourself agreeing with any of the following statements?

➡ 'I control my emotions by not expressing them.'

➡ 'When I am feeling negative emotions, I make sure not to express them.'

➡ 'I keep my emotions to myself.'

Try especially to think back to times when you felt bad but were around other people. Do the statements describe you at all? If that's you, you might be well served by trying to train yourself in the use of reappraisal instead.

Remember that the point of techniques such as reappraisal is that they help to keep us on track. When we've had a train wreck of a day – say we succumbed to temptation or got knocked back from our goals – such techniques can help us to keep our mistakes and failures in perspective. Rather than letting bad moods get the better of us, we can wrest control back from our emotions and get on course with our goals again.

An ex-colleague and friend called Raina decided last year that she wanted to move on from a somewhat abusive relationship. The break-up has been very acrimonious and lawyers are still arguing about the division of the home that they co-own. She realises that she will eventually be better off, but that doesn't make the split any easier.

We catch up periodically for what we call peer coaching sessions – giving each other advice on both our professional and personal lives. Naturally, we begin by exchanging pleasantries. I ask her how she is and she often replies, 'Oh, fine, thanks.'

But I know Raina too well. When I can see it on her face and hear the tone in her voice that she's far from 'fine', I gently chide her. I remind her that it's not healthy to bottle up her emotions all of the time. She's a psychologist, but even psychologists need reminding occasionally. She may need to do so with mere acquaintances or friends she doesn't know well. But I remind her that she needn't do so – and *mustn't* do so – with her good friends.

ANNOUNCING HOW WE'D LIKE TO FEEL

What about some other popular methods for managing our emotions? How well do they work?

A client once came to me for guidance because she was severely lacking in confidence. She wanted – no, *needed* – to alter not only how she felt about herself but also how she came across to colleagues. Victoria was a young woman in her late thirties with a petite frame and long pumpkin-coloured hair falling in waves past her shoulders. She worked as a business development manager – a salesperson, essentially – for a plastics and chemicals manufacturer. Her job was to be charismatic and persuasive when dealing with customers, which wasn't a problem for her. Despite the fact that many of her customers were older and more experienced than her, she said she enjoyed that aspect of her job and coped well with it.

Somewhat surprisingly, though, she felt almost crippling levels of self-doubt when dealing with her colleagues. She hated meetings and worried constantly about having to say anything at all. During meetings at which she knew she would have to provide updates to the team, she sometimes felt so nervous that she fought the urge to be physically sick.

While she had never felt particularly confident about speaking up in front of people, she felt that the problem had worsened relatively recently when the company hit a bad patch and some of her colleagues lost their jobs. The added worry that a wrong comment on her part might put her in the firing line tipped her over the edge from feeling apprehensive to almost being blinded by fear.

There was another contributing factor too. She had been put in charge of a team of three junior salespeople, but the members of her team had swiftly established that she was a walkover. They no longer respected her and one of her team was almost openly hostile to her. Taking everything together, she was quite distressed about her work.

I began by quizzing her about what else she might have tried to boost her confidence. She responded that she frequently repeated positive statements or affirmations. Whenever she was feeling afraid or insecure, she would repeat a positive phrase about how she wanted to feel. For example, before going into a team meeting at work, she would hide in a toilet cubicle and – after checking that no one else was around who could overhear her – tell herself something like, 'I am confident. I am competent, professional and respected by my colleagues.'

Or if she had time in the morning before leaving the house for work, she might sit in front of the mirror at her dressing table and say, 'I am intelligent. I am strong, resourceful and determined. I can do anything that I put my mind to.'

Hearing her answer, I gently suggested that she might get more benefit from some other techniques. Given that she was feeling so fragile, I didn't mention that her affirmations might have done more harm than good.

The evidence suggesting that affirmations may not be beneficial for everybody comes from an elegant study by a team of psychologists led by Joanne Wood, a rising star in the field of social psychology at the University of Waterloo in Ontario. To begin, the researchers sought volunteers to complete a questionnaire that measured self-esteem. Once they'd analysed the data, they divided their volunteers into three groups. One group comprised the people who were in the top third in terms of their self-esteem scores. A second group comprised those who'd scored in the bottom third on the self-esteem test. The final group who scored in the middle of the range were excused from the rest of the experiment. So the researchers were left with two groups, each made up of individuals with either fairly high or low self-esteem.

Wood and her colleagues then explained the next part of the experiment: the participants would spend four minutes writing down their thoughts. It was up to the participants what they wrote about. However, they were told that a bell would ring occasionally and, each time it did, they should repeat to themselves the phrase 'I am a lovable person'. During the four minutes, the bell rang a total of 16 times.

After writing out their thoughts (and chanting 'I am a lovable person' numerous times), the participants completed a second range of questionnaires to measure their mood, optimism and self-esteem. So how did the phrase affect the participants?

Wood and her team discovered that the phrase – the positive affirmation – had very different effects for the two groups. The group who had been chosen initially for their high levels of self-esteem gained a boost in their mood after repeating the phrase. Unfortunately, the group with low self-esteem to begin with got worse. They felt sadder and less optimistic.

'When people are insecure and unsure of themselves, using affirmations may make them feel worse'

Delving further, the researchers asked other colleagues to analyse the lists of thoughts that the two groups had put together. Neither of these colleagues were told who had written which essays, but they spotted a trend. Those with high self-esteem often wrote about how lovable they were. In contrast, those with low self-esteem were much more likely to say that they were unlovable. Repeating the phrase 'I am a lovable person' had not helped the low self-esteem participants – it had only made them question their own appeal and devastated the little self-confidence they had.[31]

To sum up, then: affirmations may help people to feel better when they are *already* confident about themselves and what they can achieve. But when people are insecure and unsure of themselves, using affirmations may make them feel worse: sadder, less optimistic and even more doubting of their own abilities.

Returning to my client Victoria, it was clear to me that she was someone who suffered from quite low self-esteem. She compared herself very negatively to the people around her, so repeating a positive mantra of any sort was probably doing her confidence no favours. Each time she reiterated a phrase such as 'I am strong', it may have made her subconscious mind worry and question 'Am I really strong?' Saying 'I am confident' may have led her to wonder 'But I'm not confident, am I?' Rather than buoying her up, it may unknowingly have stripped away the little remaining confidence she had.

OVER TO YOU

Perhaps the most popularly repeated affirmation used by fans of the technique is 'Every day, in every way, I'm getting better and better'. Coined in the early twentieth century by a French pharmacist by the name of Émile Coué, it's a lovely sentiment. Unfortunately, modern science tells us that it may not be universally helpful. More insidiously, it may be downright dangerous for some people.

When we're trying to modify aspects of our situations, our attitudes or our lives, we will necessarily bump up against obstacles. We may make mistakes, encounter rejection and falter occasionally. That's life, right? Proponents of positive affirmations suggest repeating phrases like 'I am not afraid. I am enjoying my new feelings of calm and joy' to overcome negative emotions. But whether we should use such statements to buoy our confidence hinges upon how generally positive we feel about ourselves.

If you think of yourself as an entirely strong, confident, competent person, then by all means choose positive affirmations that you can use. However, if you think of yourself as someone who is more self-doubting, worried and apprehensive about your own talents and abilities, then you may be much better served sticking with some of the other techniques within this chapter, such as affect labelling or reappraisal.

Joanne Wood and her fellow researchers summarised their findings succinctly in the title of their published paper: 'Positive Self-Statements: Power for Some, Peril for Others'. The question is, are you one of the *some* or one of the *others*?

If you're not sure if you're high or low on self-esteem – or somewhere in the middle – here's your opportunity to find out. The following statements are taken from arguably the most popularly used test of self-esteem.[32] Work through the statements in turn and indicate the extent of your agreement with each one.

	Strongly agree	Agree	Disagree	Strongly disagree
1. I feel that I am a person of worth, at least on an equal plane with others.				
2. I feel that I have a number of good qualities.				
3. All in all, I am inclined to feel that I am a failure.				
4. At times I think I am no good at all.				
5. I am able to do things as well as most other people.				
6. I feel I do not have much to be proud of.				
7. I take a positive attitude towards myself.				
8. On the whole, I am satisfied with myself.				
9. I certainly feel useless at times.				
10. I wish I could have more respect for myself.				

For statements 1, 2, 5, 7 and 8, give yourself points as follows:

➡ 'Strongly agree' = 3

➡ 'Agree' = 2

➡ 'Disagree' = 1

➡ 'Strongly disagree' = 0

For statements 3, 4, 6, 9 and 10, the statements are phrased negatively and the scoring works the other way around. So give yourself points as follows:

➡ 'Strongly agree' = 0

➡ 'Agree' = 1

➡ 'Disagree' = 2

➡ 'Strongly disagree' = 3

Adding up your scores for all 10 statements should give you a score between 0 and 30. Scores between 15 and 25 are considered fairly ordinary; 26 and above is a sign of unreservedly high self-esteem. And a score of 14 or less might indicate low self-esteem, which suggests that using affirmations may not be your best bet for boosting your mood and confidence in the face of adversity.

HELPING OURSELVES ALONG WITH SELF-TALK *THAT WORKS*

In the interests of improving ourselves and changing our circumstances, we may unavoidably need to carry out tasks that we find less than pleasurable. Of course, we want every tool at our disposal to get through such times. But if self-affirmations don't work, what does?

I've scrutinised the instructions in self-help books and on positive thinking websites that advocate positive affirmations and noticed that their advice is typically to focus on what you want or how you wish you could be. For example, someone who is nervous about meeting new people but who wants more social confidence might be taught to say something like, 'I am fascinating and a brilliant conversationalist.' An individual who is overweight and wants to slim down might repeat, 'I am athletic. I am the perfect weight and make healthy choices in life.'

The advice is usually to repeat positive affirmations in the present tense as if you have *already* attained the feelings or achievements you want. So a budding entrepreneur who wants to make lots of money might say, 'I am rich,' rather than 'I will be rich.' Somebody on the lookout for love might say, 'I have a wonderful partner and we are both happy and at peace.'

The study by the researcher Joanne Wood tells us that such broad claims don't benefit everybody. If you think about it, people who are low on self-confidence know that they're nervous and not great conversationalists; that they're very unhappy about their weight and not athletic; that they are barely making ends meet and far from being wealthy. Perhaps it's the fact that they see through their own positive claims that makes them feel worse.

However, there is verifiable evidence suggesting that more *specific*, targeted phrases may goad us on when things are tough. Veteran researcher Ute Bayer and a colleague at the University of Konstanz in Germany recruited 40 students to take part in an important experiment on the effects of positive phrases on performance in a mathematics test.

The test consisted of 14 mathematical problems and the participants were given only 10 minutes to solve as many of them as they could. To test the effects of different positive phrases on performance, the researchers split the 40 students into two groups.

The first group was told to focus on a positively phrased goal: 'I will correctly solve as many problems as possible!' Yes, the instruction even included the exclamation mark – as if including it could make mathematics more fun, perhaps?

The second group was told to think about the same positively phrased goal: 'I will correctly solve as many problems as possible!' However, they were also asked to read and reflect upon a second sentence: 'And if I start a new problem, then I will tell myself: I can solve it!'

Both groups were given three minutes to mull over their instructions before taking the fiendishly challenging test. I say that the test was difficult because participants in the first group (who were told to concentrate on the single phrase 'I will correctly solve as many problems as possible!') only solved an average of 2.8 problems correctly. Given that there were 14 problems in total, that only translates into a measly 20 per cent. Really not a fantastic performance.

However, participants in the second group who were given the additional instruction 'And if I start a new problem, then I will tell myself: I can solve it!' solved an average of 4.3 problems correctly. That's a score of 31 per cent, which is a marked improvement over the first group.[33]

What happened? Why did the extra sentence make such a big difference?

Let's read that second sentence again more carefully: 'And if I start a new problem, then I will tell myself: I can solve it!' Does it remind you of anything? Of the implementation intentions that we encountered back in Chapter Two: Setting Effective Goals, perhaps?

Because that's exactly what it is: an implementation intention.* The additional sentence says that when a participant starts a new problem, he or she will say – perhaps muttering under their breath or silently in their heads, we don't know which – 'I can solve it!' It's the same as an individual who wants to quit smoking saying, 'When I feel the craving for a cigarette when I'm out with friends, I will chew a piece of gum,' or somebody who wants to avoid getting angry when stressed making the plan, 'If I feel myself getting hacked off with a colleague, I will excuse myself and walk around the office for 60 seconds.' These are all specific plans to behave in a particular way when a certain set of circumstances arises.

'Self-talk that focuses on *how* we can conquer a specific ordeal seems to boost performance'

Saying 'I can solve it!' when encountering a mathematical quandary is similar to the specific, positive self-talk that athletes use to boost their performance during sporting competitions. For example, a 100-metre runner might say, 'I will run as fast as my personal best,' while a gymnast might repeatedly declare, 'I will pull my knees into my chest as tightly as possible to somersault into the air.'

---

* See the section 'From intention to implementation' starting on page 49 if you want a refresher about implementation intentions.

There are two points that you as a discerning reader might take away from Ute Bayer's study. First of all, self-talk that focuses on *how* we can conquer a specific ordeal seems to boost performance. A nervous job-hunter going into an interview might verbalise the thought, 'I will smile and exude confidence during this interview.' A salesperson wanting to negotiate a profitable deal with a customer might say, 'I will ask lots of questions and paraphrase to show that I comprehend the customer's needs.' The emphasis is on specific behaviours – smiling and exuding confidence or asking questions and paraphrasing. And it focuses on that *particular* interview, a *specific* business meeting, or whatever the *precise* situation might be. That's very different from the sentiment behind broad positive affirmations such as 'I am rich' or 'I have a partner who loves me' when you're actually on the poverty line or unhappily single – these are really no more than wishes or hopes.

Secondly, it's making the plan to use them – by constructing an implementation intention – that helps us to remember to use them. You may recall that having an intention doesn't always translate into action. It seems to be planning when and how we're going to take action that prompts us to follow through.

OVER TO YOU

The participants in Ute Bayer's profoundly important study benefited in their mathematics test by spending a mere three minutes focusing not only on their goal (i.e. to improve their performance) but also a specific implementation intention about how they would repeat a can-do phrase to themselves. Three minutes isn't long if we want to improve our performance in all sorts of situations – from giving a speech at a friend's wedding and chatting to strangers at parties, to asserting ourselves with colleagues and even doing well when we're playing sports or games.

To me, there seem to be two essential steps to preparing to use positive self-talk effectively.

One, sit down and think about the *specific situation* in which you want to perform well. So that might be the weekly meeting that you attend at work – and the next one is this Friday. Or that might be a party on Saturday evening or your driving test in just over two weeks' time on the 21st of the month.

Next, think about the *specific behaviours* you want to demonstrate in that situation. Avoid broad generalisations like 'I want to be successful in getting the bank manager to give me a loan,' or 'I will be charming and funny at the party.' Think about what you will do or say in order to achieve unbridled success in those situations. For example, that might be 'I will speak slowly in an authoritative voice when meeting the bank manager,' or 'I will compliment people and poke fun at myself during the party.'

Earlier this year, I coached an affable company director called Sergio who was keen to review his work–life balance. His wife was undergoing treatment for breast cancer and he wanted to be more supportive of her, even if it meant de-emphasising his own career. But first we looked at ways for him to claw back more time away from the office by being more productive.

After only a little discussion, he realised that he frequently got invited to meetings that were only tangentially relevant to his own work. Saying 'no' more often and turning some of them down would allow him to get more of his own work done. At other times, he wanted to say that he would only stay for the portion of any meeting that was directly pertinent to him. Doing so helped to free up at least several hours every week. But being more assertive in face-to-face situations wasn't something that came easily to someone as obliging as Sergio. So he put together several positive phrases to bolster his confidence:

➡ 'When people ask for my involvement in projects, I will tell myself that I have the right to say no.'

➡ 'I will explain to people when I have important phone calls to make.'

The first phrase, for example, allowed a little time for him to go away and weigh up whether any project was important and relevant to his role as opposed to being perhaps interesting but less critical. The second phrase reminded him to put his own work first rather than being too helpful to his colleagues.

Sergio gradually discovered that standing his ground helped him to free up more time every week. More importantly, he was getting just as much of his own work done *and* getting away from the office earlier.

In striving to make change happen in our own lives, we all may at least occasionally have tasks to complete that might be less than entirely enjoyable. At such times, thinking ahead about a phrase or two of positive self-talk that we could use *during* such tasks could make a difference.

EXERCISING OUR EMOTIONS

In the Introduction, I recounted that getting fit had changed my life. Pounding a treadmill and throwing weights around in a gym had altered not only my body but also how I felt about myself. It was such a startling transformation that I became a bit of an exercise evangelist, wanting to convert everyone around me.

I decided to spend three years researching the topic of physical exercise for my doctorate. In reviewing the literature on the subject, I discovered the power of physical exercise to boost people's moods – even when those people have been diagnosed by mental-health experts with what's known as major depressive disorder.

In a study that shocked the medical community at the time, a crack team of a dozen doctors, psychologists and other behavioural researchers led by James Blumenthal at Duke Medical Center in North Carolina set out to compare the effectiveness of physical exercise versus antidepressant medication for treating depression. Blumenthal is an impeccably credentialed clinical psychologist who continues to spend his career investigating the links between physical and mental health. Back in 1999, he and his team tried something that no one else had ever tried: they took more than 100 adults who had been diagnosed with depression and randomly assigned them either a programme of moderate aerobic exercise or treatment with a proven antidepressant drug. Which would turn out to be the better cure?

Depending on their level of fitness, the patients who were ordered to exercise either walked or jogged. Irrespective of what they did, they all exercised three times a week, for 45 minutes on each occasion.

The scientific team monitored the patients in the two groups for four months and found . . . well, what do you think they observed? Which treatment would you think was the more effective?

The researchers found that both treatments were *equally* effective. As expected, the antidepressant medication success-fully lifted the mood of the patients who received it. However, physical exercise had exactly the same benefit.

That's a rather profound result that deserves a little more discussion.

Remember that the participants in the study weren't merely a bit low or moderately unhappy. They had been categorised as having a depressive disorder – a clinical syndrome characterised by total apathy, the inability to experience pleasure and, in many cases, thoughts of suicide. The doctors were sufficiently worried about their well-being that the patients would otherwise have been prescribed medication and put under observation.

In comparison, the exercise wasn't excessively strenuous. Some of the depressed patients weren't fit enough to jog and were only allowed to walk at a brisk pace to get their hearts racing. And they exercised for fewer than three hours a week – less than the average person spends watching TV *in a single day*.[34] Yet exercise was as successful at lifting their mood as medication – a treatment that's expensive, requires expert medical supervision and sometimes has side effects ranging from constipation and loss of sex drive to headaches and weight gain.[35]

You can imagine that Blumenthal and his team were rather bewildered. Some of the doctors on his team checked and re-checked their data to make sure they hadn't made a mistake. But the results were strikingly clear: physical exercise – an activity no more complicated than gentle jogging or brisk walking – was enough to the lift the cloud of clinical depression.

Neither was this study a one-off, a statistical anomaly. Dozens of studies on the subject have since been conducted, all of them leading to the same conclusion. In fact, more recent research suggests that exercise may not only treat depression – it may help to alleviate anxiety disorders too. There's also evidence that exercise may not just treat but even *prevent* mental disorders.[36]

But this chapter is about techniques that can help us to build greater emotional resilience and bolster our chances of making change happen – to bounce back after a rejection, disappointment, mistake or failure. So how can exercise help?

In one study that I completed as part of my doctorate under the guidance of David Hemsley, a distinguished professor at the Institute of Psychiatry in London, I found that even a single session of exercise can lift mood. Taking a group of healthy but in some cases overweight volunteers, I randomly assigned them to engage in either a workout or a period of quiet relaxation for the same length of time.

'Even a single session of exercise can lift mood'

By asking everyone to complete questionnaires about how they felt after either the workout or relaxation, I found that people who engaged in just one stint of exercise felt more energetic, alert and exhilarated – significantly more so than the people who sat relaxing silently. If the exercisers felt upset or at all distressed beforehand, they felt significantly less so afterwards too.[37]

OVER TO YOU

So far, the techniques I've covered in this chapter have been quite cerebral in nature. They involve naming the emotions we're feeling or trying to view our circumstances differently. But sometimes when we're feeling particularly overwrought – perhaps on the verge of tears or literally shaking with fury – it can be hard to break free of our feelings by relying only on cognitive techniques. Physical exercise may be a useful alternative for rebooting how we feel.

You don't have to be a member of a gym or even put on a pair of running shoes. If you aren't very fit, take a brisk walk around the block. Climb up and down a flight of stairs a handful of times. Play tennis on a Wii or the Xbox Kinect. Put on your favourite song and dance around your bedroom. As little as 10 minutes is enough to get the psychological benefits.[38]

Do something – anything – that gets your body warm and makes you a little out of breath. It almost doesn't matter what you do, as exercise lifts our mood for a couple of reasons. For a start, it distracts us from worrying thoughts. It's hard to dwell on past mistakes or future concerns when we're sweating and out of breath. What's more, exercise may release endorphins – natural feel-good chemicals that are biochemically related to cocaine and heroin – into the bloodstream, and these hit the mood centres of our brains.[39]

ONWARDS AND UPWARDS

➡ Remember that mistakes, knock-backs and even outright failures are a natural – or maybe even essential – part of making change happen. Few people who decide to alter their lives get everything without stumbling at least a little. The important thing is to keep trying.

➡ Keep in mind the distinction between healthy and unhealthy negative emotions. While it's natural to feel emotions such as sadness, guilt and annoyance, we must be careful not to get so overwrought that we can't resume pursuit of our goals.

➡ Help yourself to ward off negative emotions by using the technique of affect labelling. Simply describe the situation you're in to get some clarity on what's happening. Doing so should help to blunt the force of jarring emotions.

➡ Try reappraisal to re-construe the situations you're in too. Pushing yourself to find alternative explanations and different meanings within situations is an even more potent tool for helping you to reassert control over your emotions.

➡ Be careful about using broad positive affirmations; they only work if you are feeling fairly confident and upbeat to begin with. But do boost your performance and mood in challenging situations with positive, task-specific self-talk (backed up by an implementation intention to use it in the first place).

➡ And if you're looking for an instant way to boost your mood, do some physical exercise. It may reboot how you're feeling and make you feel more positive.

SIX

TAPPING INTO PEOPLE POWER

'Consult your friend on all things, especially on those which respect yourself. His counsel may then be useful where your own self-love might impair your judgement.'

Lucius Annaeus Seneca

A client called Annabel once wanted to find a new direction and purpose in life. A slight and quietly spoken woman with neatly coiffed platinum-blonde hair who turned 50 last year, she told me that she had recently split from her husband. Like many couples, they had adopted traditional roles within the family: she stayed at home to bring up their children while her husband worked. But when her grown-up daughter and two sons left home, she found herself living with someone who felt more like an acquaintance than a spouse. After more than two decades together, she felt so isolated and lonely within her marriage that she asked for a divorce.

The dissolution of her marriage was extremely harrowing and emotionally bruising. Her husband acted bitterly and her younger son sided with him, telling her that she was selfish for breaking up the family. But she ultimately prevailed.

When she eventually found herself newly single, she sought to grow her self-confidence and find an identity that didn't revolve around being a wife and mother. Part of this involved wanting to find a new career or vocation. She was also looking for a new partner in life, a man with whom she could share fresh adventures.

Placing an advert in the dating section of a respectable newspaper, she was both pleased and surprised to receive dozens of replies from men interested in meeting her. She was naturally more than a little nervous at the prospect of dating – she'd been with her husband for more than a quarter of a century. But she decided to do it anyway.

Those first steps on the dating scene took place nearly two years ago. Today, she spends rather a lot of time with a captivating man called Randolph. He runs an engineering business and is a keen horticulturalist but, more importantly, he finds Annabel ceaselessly entertaining. Best of all, she feels the same about him.

That sounds straightforward enough, but it wasn't. Far from it. Although she went on several dates arranged through the matchmaking service, she ultimately came to the conclusion that it wasn't for her – she opined that it might suit a younger generation, but not a traditionalist like herself.

No, she met Randolph at a wine-tasting evening that she attended on the suggestion of a friend. Indeed, many of the good ideas and support that she received came from the people around her – friends, family and even more casual acquaintances. Friends gave Annabel advice on buying brand new clothes that suited a newly single woman in her middle years. Others buoyed her confidence during the dark moments when she worried that she had done the wrong thing in divorcing her husband.

Further friends organised lunches, dinners, brunches and picnics and invited eligible bachelors along; they enrolled with her in evening classes so she wouldn't have to meet new people entirely on her own. They cheered her dating successes and commiserated with her when things didn't go well. Her web of supporters helped her in so many ways – and I've not even mentioned how they assisted her with her job-hunt.

It may sound as if Annabel was fortunate because she had a supersized social network. But she didn't. Like most people, she had a small circle of close friends and a larger – but by no means immense – circle of more casual friends and acquaintances. However, she managed to mobilise so many of them to advise her, guide her and urge her on.

> 'Friends, family and social connections are amongst the largest resources upon which we can draw when we're trying to make change happen'

Research shows that our friends, family and social connections are amongst the largest resources upon which we can draw when we're trying to make change happen in our lives. Having the right people around us can bestow us with both emotional support and practical assistance. Even better, it turns out that we can draw upon the support of friends we've yet to meet – including celebrities and people in the public eye whom we may *never* meet. And in this chapter I'll tell you exactly how.

APPRECIATING THE CONTAGIOUSNESS OF CHANGE

A growing body of evidence suggests that having the right people around us can make a big difference in whether we successfully manage to change or not. That may not sound like a particularly controversial statement. Having someone in the same situation – who's experiencing similar problems or issues – can be terribly comforting. It's natural to want kind, supportive people around us who can encourage or even advise us.

However, the science throws up a snag: the people we're most likely to turn to may not always help us to achieve our goals. At times, our most compassionate friends and accommodating relatives may even hamper us from changing successfully.

The scientific evidence comes from research started way back in 1948. Just after the end of the Second World War, the National Heart Institute (now called the National Heart, Lung and Blood Institute) in the US began what has become a landmark study looking into the factors or characteristics that contribute to heart disease. The groundbreaking team of researchers recruited a group – or what's known in research circles as a cohort – of 5,209 men and women between the ages of 30 and 62 from the town of Framingham in Massachusetts to take part in their study. Every few years, the investigators brought the participants into their laboratory to weigh, measure and test them. For decades, the researchers noted their weights and heights. They took measurements of blood pressure and collected blood samples to test blood triglyceride and cholesterol levels. And they asked the participants lots and lots of questions about what they ate, how they spent their spare time – even whom they spent time with and how they felt about their lives.

'Our most compassionate friends and accommodating relatives may even hamper us from changing successfully'

Since its inception, the Framingham Heart Study has made major contributions to the medical profession's grasp of what causes heart disease. The scope of the study has expanded to include many other diseases too. In fact, the study has become one of the world's largest and most rigorous investigations looking at the factors that lead to good (and bad) health in general.

But it's not the original group of participants that we're interested in for now. In 1971, the researchers began a second phase of the research, successfully persuading most of the children of the original cohort as well as these children's spouses that they too should be prodded and probed over the course of their lifetimes. Over the next 30 years, these grown-up children and their spouses spread out all across the United States but continued to participate in the project, allowing the researchers to weigh, measure and question them until 2002.

By following up this second cohort, the researchers were able to gather huge tomes of information on a social network of 12,067 people over the course of more than 30 years. You can see how that amounts to a mammoth data set. Analysing this very large set of records, healthcare policy researcher Nicholas Christakis and a colleague at Harvard Medical School were able to discern some of the causes and interrelationships that lead to clinical obesity.

The researchers determined that a person's chances of becoming obese over this 30-year period was significantly influenced by the number of obese people in that individual's life. For example, someone with a friend who originally wasn't obese but who became obese was in turn 57 per cent more likely to become obese too.

Analysing the data in more depth, the investigators found that the gender of the two friends was a significant factor. Having a friend of the opposite gender become obese made no difference to an individual's chances of becoming obese. But having a same-sex friend become obese meant a whopping 71 per cent increase in the chances that the individual would later become obese too.

The implication for the rest of us is a little shocking: if one of our same-sex friends were to put on lots of weight – or already has done in the time we've known them – then our odds of ballooning shoots up by 71 per cent too. No matter how outwardly supportive they might be of our attempts to lose weight or keep weight off, their mere presence in our social circles alters our chances of success.

Perhaps surprisingly, the effects of having a husband or wife become obese were actually less than those of having an obese friend. A woman whose husband became obese was 37 per cent more likely to become obese subsequently. A man whose wife became obese was 44 per cent more likely to become obese too.[40]

The precise percentages are less important than the overall conclusions of the study. Just as diseases ranging from malaria to the common cold are passed from one person to the next, obesity is *socially transmitted*. We are all socially connected and so is our health.

The researchers eliminated other possible causes. They found that weight gain wasn't down to the food that was on offer at local supermarkets or restaurants, or the proximity of exercise facilities such as the nearest park or swimming pool. It wasn't about the ease with which people could drive to work versus having opportunities to walk.

Simply being with friends who are obese seems to alter our attitudes and behaviour. A much heavier friend may be less likely to slate us when our willpower buckles and we opt for the burger and chips instead of the grilled chicken breast and salad. When we hang around with more people who are overweight, we may subconsciously see it as more socially acceptable to be overweight too.

But it's not just obesity that jumps from friend to friend or spouse to spouse. Similar research by J. Niels Rosenquist, a psychiatrist at Massachusetts General Hospital, tells us that spending time with heavy drinkers makes us more prone to drink too much as well.[41] Spend our weekends with abstemious friends who favour mineral water over hard liquor and of course we're going to hold back. But go out with hard partiers who like to chase their beer with whisky shots and we'll undoubtedly feel the pressure to drink more.

The same, it turns out, is true of smoking. Spending time with smokers makes it harder for us to quit smoking.[42]

Take my friend Fenella, for instance. Coming up to her thirtieth birthday, she had been smoking for nearly half of her life, around 20 cigarettes a day. She had never previously been someone who was tormented by the health risks of smoking – she saw it as a relatively minor vice that helped her to cope with the stresses of a high-powered job in publishing. On the cusp of turning 30, though, she was beginning to worry about her appearance.

Of Indian descent, she has long black hair, a strong nose and an unlined face that looks considerably younger. But she wanted to stay young-looking. She had her teeth bleached a couple of months ago and was already deliberating over the benefits of Botox injections. Nevertheless, she began to appreciate that giving up smoking might help her to prolong her looks.

She used nicotine gum briefly, as well as a nicotine inhaler, and succeeded in quitting smoking. Most of her friends were surprised at her discipline, and pleased too. At least that was the story six months ago.

When I met up with Fenella recently, she had started smoking again. Why? I wanted to know how she'd slipped back into her bad habits.

'My friend Beth from university who moved back to Canada came to stay with me for a few weeks. She always went outside into the garden to smoke but I'd have a couple of cigarettes with her to keep her company,' she told me.

And that was all it took. Even when Beth left, Fenella unfortunately carried on smoking. Just a few weeks spent with a close friend who smoked was enough to undo all her good work.

MAKING HARD DECISIONS

It's not only our health that is affected by the people around us. Almost all of our choices are affected by the people with whom we choose to associate. For example, it turns out that our mood – our very happiness – is at least partly determined by how the people around us feel too.

As part of the Framingham Heart Study, the many thousands of participants were asked questions about their level of happiness. Given statements such as 'I feel hopeful about the future' and 'I am happy', the participants rated themselves on scales ranging from 0 (for 'rarely or none of the time') to 3 ('most or all of the time'). Analysing the data, behavioural scientist James Fowler at University of California, San Diego, and Nicholas Christakis (who led the analysis of the obesity study we discussed earlier) analysed changes in happiness over the course of several decades. Rather than looking simply at clusters of happy or unhappy people, the enquiring researchers were able to see how happiness spread over time. Over the period from 1996 to 2000, for example, 16 per cent of the participants said that they became happy while 13 per cent became unhappy. What led to these changes?

'Our mood – our very happiness – is at least partly determined by how the people around us feel too'

The biggest factor was having a friend who became happy living a mile (about 1.6 km) or less away, which increased the likelihood of an individual becoming happy by 25 per cent.[43] Friends who lived too far away had little effect on happiness, which suggests that being able to spend time with a happy friend makes us happy too. We see much more of friends who live locally, so they naturally have the greatest impact on our happiness or unhappiness. Even though we may care deeply for our friends who live further away, the distance means that our lives may be less closely intertwined and, as such, our happiness may be less dependent on each other's too.

The point of such studies is that our ability to modify our lives in a sustainable fashion is at least to some extent determined by the people we choose to have in our lives. Making conscious decisions about the people we spend time with can accelerate our progress towards our goals. That may mean investing more time with certain people; perhaps we can pick up practical tips or simply absorb some of their positive attitude. At the same time, though, that may mean deliberately deciding to reduce the amount of time we spend with others, perhaps because they have lifestyles or attitudes that aren't helpful to our particular goals.

'Elect to spend more time with the right people and you help yourself to make change happen'

That may sound like a cold, calculating proposition. But remember that this isn't my personal opinion about what we need to do. This is a recommendation based on research. Science doesn't tell us what the warm and fuzzy option might be – it simply tells us the reality of what occurs. And the truth is this: elect to spend more time with the right people and you help yourself to make change happen.

OVER TO YOU

Several dozen studies tell us that our behaviour, lifestyles, aspirations and even mental attitudes such as happiness can be socially transmitted. If you think about it, it makes total sense. Hang around with people who play football and you're more likely to give it a go too. Or if you want to learn a new language like French or Mandarin Chinese, you're more likely to pick up the language if you know or can find your way to people who speak French or Mandarin Chinese. Whether consciously or subconsciously, we are influenced by the people around us. We gamble our futures constantly based on the company we keep.

The research also has a warning for us. Spending time with other people who want (but who have not yet achieved) the changes we desire in life may not necessarily be the best option for us. Suppose, for instance, that you want to lose weight. Joining a weight-loss club at which everyone else is currently overweight may impart a false sense of security – the other members of the club may be warm, welcoming and supportive. But it's actually associating with more people who have *already successfully lost weight* – emphasis on the past tense – that will boost your chances of losing weight too.

If you're unemployed and looking for a job, seek the company of people who are already in employment. The chances are they will have more advice and better contacts than people who are similarly out of work. Or if you want to start a business, get yourself introduced to successful business owners and entrepreneurs – not people who simply wish they could strike out on their own too.

The flip side of the equation is that we may sometimes need to distance ourselves from people who don't have the right lifestyles or attitudes. If you're trying to boost your confidence or mood, then spending time with very anxious or depressed individuals could drag you down, for instance. Alcoholics Anonymous advocates severing all ties with people who drink too much, although that may be an extreme point of view. For many of us, it simply isn't practicable to ditch friends and shun family members. But it might make us think twice about whom we call or accept invitations from whenever it's feasible.

I once coached a manager called Carina who had the fast-talking intensity of a teenager after too many cans of Red Bull. She originally sought guidance on dealing with some nasty office politics at the food and drinks company where she worked.

During the course of our discussions, she revealed that she had started experiencing panic attacks a few years ago. That and a perennially elevated level of anxiety that bubbled away in her mind meant that she had seen a psychotherapist for a while and was still taking a low dose of a medication that a doctor had prescribed for her.

She mentioned that she was spending a lot of time supporting a friend who was suffering from depression. They had initially bonded over their mutual mental-health issues but her friend was becoming more and more reliant on her. Carina was somehow personal assistant, confidant, mother and therapist to her friend; Carina sometimes bought groceries for her, cooked for her, and had on several occasions stayed up all night comforting her increasingly dependent friend.

Carina's concern was that the rollercoaster of her friend's emotions wasn't good for either of them. Indeed, Carina's anxiety had worsened in recent months and her doctor had increased the dosage of her anti-anxiety medication.

'What should I do?' she asked.

'What do *you* think you should do?' I replied.

Carina was worried about being 'selfish' and 'letting down' her friend. But she knew the answer: she needed to put her own health first. She simply couldn't devote as much time to looking after her friend as her friend wanted. Being an emotional crutch for her friend wasn't helping either of them.

She eventually explained to her friend that she was worried about both of their recoveries. Gradually, she encouraged and sometimes gently insisted that her friend turn to other friends, family members and doctors for help rather than always relying on Carina for everything. Ultimately, Carina made enough progress in sorting out her own work and personal life that she was able to come off her anti-anxiety medication entirely.

ASKING AND RECEIVING

There's another way we can get our friends to help us. But to explain, let me first ask you a somewhat strange question: how likely is it that you will floss your teeth in the next two weeks?

That was precisely the question that Columbia University behavioural scientist Jonathan Levav and a colleague asked some business students – or at least *one* group of students. A second group of students was asked how likely they were to read for pleasure over the same period of time.

Two weeks later, the same participants were asked to report how many times they had actually flossed. The participants who'd been asked to predict their likelihood of flossing did so on average 6.25 times, while those who'd been asked the control question about reading flossed only 4.11 times.

The researchers attribute the finding to what's been called the 'mere measurement effect'. Simply asking people a question about their intentions to behave in a certain way makes it more likely that they will actually perform that behaviour.

Hold on a moment, though. A critic might argue that the experiment only demonstrates that reminding people about a behaviour makes them more likely to do it. But that's not the case, as the researchers had actually included a third group who were asked to indicate the likelihood that one of their classmates would floss his or her teeth in the next two weeks.

This question reminds people about flossing too – albeit indirectly – but didn't result in any appreciable rise in the number of times the students flossed two weeks later. Participants in this third group flossed 4.23 times, which was statistically no different to the 4.11 times flossed by the participants who'd been asked about reading.[44] This suggests that simply mentioning an action such as flossing isn't enough to modify someone's behaviour; it's asking someone a question about their intention to perform the behaviour that makes the difference.

Neither is it a small difference. Asking people about their intentions resulted in the participants flossing over 50 per cent more.

Psychologists contend that being asked a question about our behaviour may create a representation – perhaps a kind of image or mental connection – in our minds that makes it easier for us to actually perform that behaviour. This mere measurement effect has been replicated in plenty of other studies. For example, people who were asked about their intentions to vote in an upcoming county election became more likely to actually vote than people who weren't queried about their intentions.[45] And in a separate study conducted on a nationwide sample of more than 40,000 people, researchers found that Americans who were asked about their intentions to buy a car became 35 per cent more likely to purchase a car in the following six months than those who were not asked the same question.[46]

So, if you'll allow me to, I'd like to ask you a question. Will *you* put this technique into practice?

OVER TO YOU

If you want your friends to help you to achieve your goals, get them to ask you questions about *specific actions* that you would like to take. If you want to cook healthy meals at home rather than ordering in fast food, suggest that your friends ask you, 'Will you cook a healthy meal tomorrow night? What will you cook?' Or if you want to study towards a qualification that will help you to get a new job, give your loved ones permission to ask you, 'Will you study this weekend?'

We can use this technique to motivate our friends and loved ones too. Rather than nagging them by giving instructions such as 'Pick up the dry cleaning tomorrow, please', we would be better off asking them a question: 'Could you pick up the dry cleaning tomorrow, please?' Rather than telling someone to stop drinking so many sugary drinks, perhaps try asking, 'Do you think you might substitute a carbonated drink for a glass of water today?'

And we might also be more successful in changing people's behaviour by asking about their *future* intentions rather than their past behaviour. For example, a friend of mine broke her arm several months ago while ice skating. When the cast came off, she was advised to complete a set of exercises several times a day to restore both the strength and flexibility in her arm. Rather than asking her, 'Have you done your exercises recently?' I made an attempt to spur her on by asking, 'Will you do your exercises tomorrow?'

What question might you ask your friends to ask you?

Try it and see how it works. For example, I worked with someone I'll call Desmond, a softly spoken accountant within a travel company, who sought me out for help in mapping out some personal goals. With the arrival of a new, considerably younger and more aggressive boss, as well as the introduction of multiple changes to the nature of his job, the 50-something-year-old had become increasingly disenchanted with his work and wanted to craft a new life for himself. One part of his ambition was to become a writer.

He realised that writing fiction for a living would be an uphill struggle, but he was determined to include it in his life. He wanted to do it for his personal fulfilment, even if he would have to continue doing other work alongside it to pay the bills.

Like many people, Desmond often dithered and found it difficult to get started each day; he admitted to being able to find dozens of reasons to avoid sitting down at his computer in the first place.

However, he eventually found a solution that worked for him. Recruiting a group of likeminded people from the Internet, he set up a writing circle of would-be writers. He asked his confederates to phone or email him occasionally to ask, 'Will you do some writing tomorrow?' and 'How much do you think you'll get done?' In return, he did the same for them.

Desmond found that saying 'yes' and making a specific pledge as to the number of hours he would spend writing sometimes gave him the shove he needed. He felt that his answers were like a promise and, while he was more than happy to break promises to himself, he didn't like to let his fellow writers down. Granted, he didn't always manage to write as much as he assured his writing circle he would, but he wrote more than he might have done without that extra little push from them.

COLLABORATING WITH A PARTNER

Suppose you have a close friend, husband, wife or housemate who has the same goal as you. Whether you're both looking to escape tedious jobs or kick-start healthier lifestyles, that should be great, right? You can remind each other of your commitments and gee each other up when one or the other of you isn't feeling terribly motivated.

When I started hitting the gym back when I was at university, I had a gym buddy called Dave, who also studied psychology with me. We used to meet on Tuesday and Thursday evenings to play a couple of games of squash before throwing some weights around in the gym. Surely having a gym buddy helped me to stay more motivated?

Actually, it might not have done. It sounds like a sensible idea. But the research tells us that having a partner with the same goal *doesn't* necessarily help us to achieve more.

Andrew Prestwich at the Institute of Psychological Sciences at the University of Leeds was kind enough to tell me about a study that he and his colleagues published in 2012. He and his team recruited 257 local government employees into an experiment comparing the effectiveness of buddying versus working independently in the promotion of physical exercise and weight loss. He randomly assigned his participants to one of four groups, each of which was given different instructions. The first, control group was encouraged to exercise but given no further advice on how to go about it. A second group was asked to find a buddy, a partner to support them. The participants in this group were given instructions as follows:

> Past research suggests that despite intending to
> undertake more physical activity, many people fail to
> do so. To give yourself the best chance of succeeding,
> it seems that it can be helpful to recruit a partner (e.g.
> husband, wife, girlfriend, boyfriend, housemate, etc.) to
> assist you in increasing the amount of physical activity
> you do.

Six months later, the researchers asked participants in the two groups how much exercise they were doing; they also weighed the participants to see how much weight they had lost. Perhaps surprisingly, both groups were only doing slightly more exercise than they had been before the start of the study. Both groups had also lost around a kilogram in weight. But there were no differences between the two groups; they had lost almost the same amount of weight. It seemed that seeking out a partner did *not* help participants to lose more weight.

However, all is not lost. Prestwich is a canny, experienced researcher in the fields of health and social psychology so was keenly aware of the evidence regarding implementation intentions (which we came across in Chapter Two: Setting Effective Goals). So it's actually his third and fourth groups that should interest us the most.

Participants in the third group were asked to form individual implementation intentions. In other words, each person was asked to decide when and exactly how they would go about exercising.

But the real test was in a fourth group. These participants were told to concoct a series of implementation intentions *with a partner*. Here's just part of the instructions that these participants read:

> *Past research suggests that despite intending to undertake regular physical activity, many people fail to do so. To give yourself the best chance of succeeding, it seems that it can be helpful to make very specific plans with a partner (e.g. husband, wife, girlfriend, boyfriend, housemate, etc.) about how together you will go about increasing the amount of regular physical activity you do.*

Six months later, those who had been taught to form imple-mentation intentions on their own lost a little more weight. But those who formed collaborative implementation intentions with a partner lost the most weight of all – nearly three times as much weight as everyone else in the study.[47]

So allow me to spell out the implications of the study. First of all, it confirms something we already know: implementation intentions work. Making specific commitments as to when and where we will undertake particular activities helps us to achieve our goals.

In addition, the study tells us that simply finding a friend with similar aims is not automatically enough to spur us on to better results. It's only when we work together with our buddy or partner to devise specific plans – a set of collaborative imple-mentation intentions – that it helps us to achieve more.

OVER TO YOU

Of course, not every endeavour lends itself to working with a buddy. You may be the only person you know who wants to set up a business, learn to meditate or meet someone special. But if you *can* find a close friend, husband, wife or partner with the same goal, you may be able to strengthen your resolve by setting some collaborative implementation intentions.

The phrase 'collaborative implementation intention' probably overcomplicates matters. The research really just says that having a well-meaning, supportive friend in the same situation as us isn't enough. If we only have good inten-tions and vague plans to get together, that's not enough of a commitment. It's only by having concrete plans – actual times and dates in the diary – which we've decided upon with our buddy, that we get the biggest boost to our change efforts.

Having a buddy doesn't mean *all* of your goals have to be joint ones. For example, if you're trying to study more, you might find that some of the best times for you don't suit your study buddy. That's okay. Just try to find other times during the week when you might be able to meet up.

Get together with your buddy and think about when it might be enjoyable and/or convenient to engage in your chosen activities. Sit down and mutually map out your *specific* implementation intentions – deciding precisely *what* the two of you are agreeing to do and *when* you'll do it together.

And forgive me if it sounds too obvious to say, but effect-ive collaborative implementation intentions are likely to include the word 'we'. For example:

⇒ 'We will meet at eight o'clock on Monday evenings to play an hour of tennis.'

⇒ 'If it's raining on a Monday, we will still meet up and do a spinning class at the gym.'

⇒ 'We will get together every second Saturday morning to discuss new implementation intentions for the weeks ahead.'

You get the picture. (Oh, and if you need a refresher about how best to word implementation intentions, you can head back to Chapter Two: Setting Effective Goals.)

Thinking back to my own squash-and-gym buddy Dave, then, perhaps he was an effective source of motivation after all. Collaborative implementation intentions are nothing more than specific actions at agreed-upon times and dates in the diary. We had a specific plan that could be phrased as, 'If it's a Tuesday or a Thursday, we will meet at the squash court at seven o'clock and work out in the gym afterwards.' So thank you, Dave!

SEEKING SUPPORT FROM PEOPLE WE'VE NEVER MET

Our friends can help us in so many ways: to feel better when we are down and disheartened; to calm us when we're upset or feeling angry; and to offer new perspectives on the problems and issues we face. Most of us should be thankful for the support that we get from them. But wouldn't it be nice to have some *extraordinary* people to call upon too?

Take Sir Richard Branson, for example. The founder of the airlines-to-media Virgin empire has an estimated net worth of over US$4 billion, but, like most entrepreneurs, he started from humble beginnings. When he was a teenager, he started a mail-order record business, selling discounted records from the crypt of a church. It was an overnight success, but along came an unexpected postal strike that threatened to put a stop to his fledgling business.

Rather than give up, though, he had the audacity to take out a lease for a shop on London's Oxford Street. Within a year, he had made enough money to launch a record label, signing controversial acts such as the Sex Pistols and Culture Club, and ultimately selling the business to a much larger competitor for £500 million. Over the years, he has launched over 400 businesses, including a chain of gyms, a bank, a cosmetics company, and even a company that plans to offer space flights to the paying public.

Whether you're trying to revamp your personal or professional life – or perhaps both – wouldn't it be brilliant if you could seek his advice and support? To learn from him and soak up some of his determination, his charisma, his resilience? Of course it would.

Regrettably, it's improbable that we'd be able to seek his personal guidance. Richard Branson is clearly a busy man and unlikely to have the time for us. If most of us tried to get to him, we'd be lucky to speak to his executive assistant's assistant.

But that doesn't mean we can't draw on his strength in other ways. In fact, it turns out that we may be able to draw support from all sorts of people we've never met – and never will meet.

How?

'We may be able to draw support from all sorts of people we've never met'

The evidence comes from a series of studies conducted by an international collection of researchers from three of the world's leading higher education establishments – London Business School, National University of Singapore and Northwestern University in the US. In one particularly insightful study, for example, researchers invited volunteers to listen to an audio recording of an individual called

YOU CAN CHANGE YOUR LIFE

Keith talking about his day. Keith explains that he's a 30-year-old assistant professor teaching political science. In the course of the recording, he describes a lecture he gave that day, a meeting regarding a current research project and a departmental meeting with some of his professorial colleagues. Outside of his work, he talks about playing tennis with a buddy from his university days before having dinner with his children.

Unbeknownst to the volunteers, they had been randomly split into two groups. Each group was given a different set of written instructions to go alongside the recording.

The first group was asked to imagine what it might feel like to live Keith's life:

> When listening to the interview, take the perspective of the person being interviewed. Imagine what it would be like to be this person. That is, try to imagine what you would feel and think if you were that person. Try to go through a day in the life of this person as if you were that person. In your mind's eye, visualise clearly and vividly how it would feel to be that person. Try not to concern yourself with attending to all the information presented. Just imagine what you would feel if you were that person going through his day.

A second group was charged with taking a critical viewpoint about Keith:

> When listening to the interview, try to take an objective perspective. Try to be as objective as possible about what is happening to this person and what their day is like.

Try not to let yourself get caught up in imagining what this person has been through, how the person feels or what it would be like to be this person. Just listen to the information as objectively as possible.

Comparing the two sets of instructions, you'll have noticed that the first set asks participants to really inhabit Keith's psyche – to grasp what it's like to be him as thoroughly as possible. In contrast, the second paragraph mentions the word 'objective' three times; the researchers wanted the participants to distance themselves from Keith as much as possible.

Next, the unsuspecting participants were all asked to complete a surprise test. The researchers believed that one of the two sets of instructions might boost their performance. Care to hazard a guess as to which had the more beneficial effect?

The participants were given 20 minutes to answer 24 analytical problems. Now these were tough questions taken from an admissions test commonly used to select only the best students for entry into law schools. Here's an example of the kind of questions they were asked:

Buses 11, 43 and 82 make only a single trip each day and they are the only buses that passengers Alice, Harry, Charlie, Xander, Ellen, Nasreen and Guillaume can take to work.

Neither Ellen nor Guillaume are willing to take bus 11 on a day when Harry does.

Guillaume does not take bus 82 on a day when Xander does.

> *Charlie always chooses to take bus 43.*

> *When Alice and Nasreen take the same bus, they always choose bus 43 as well.*

So here's the question.

> *If Charlie, Guillaume and Bob want to travel to work together but insist on following the rules, which of the buses could they take?*

> a) *Bus 11 only*

> b) *Bus 82 only*

> c) *Bus 43 only*

> d) *Buses 82 or 43 only*

> e) *Any of the buses – 11, 43 or 82*

I've put the answer in the notes at the end of the book if you want to have a go at solving the puzzle.[48]

Totalling up the participants' scores, the researchers found that one group plainly outperformed the other. Participants in the second group who adopted the critical, objective mind-set scored 29.2 per cent on the test. But the participants who read the first paragraph and were asked to imagine what it would be like to be Keith scored 47.9 per cent – a conspicuous winner.

Why did imagining themselves having Keith's life help that group to score so much better on the test?

Remember that Keith described himself as an assistant professor. He talked about a research project and a meeting with his fellow professors. He's a professor – in other words, a smart guy.

Putting themselves into the shoes of an intelligent professor, the participants were able to perform significantly better on the test of analytical thinking than control participants who listened to the same recording but were told to think about it more objectively.

In other words, imagining what it must feel like to be someone else may help us to adopt some of that person's characteristics.

'Imagining what it must feel like to be someone else may help us to adopt some of that person's characteristics'

Interestingly enough, the effect can work both ways. It can endow us with a boost or it can backfire, depending on whom we choose to think about. In another study, for example, other participants were asked by the same researchers to reflect on what it must be like to be a cheerleader. I'm sure you can picture one now in your mind: a trim, athletic, maybe pretty girl dressed in a tight top with a short, ruffled skirt. She's wearing white socks and trainers and is waving a pair of pompoms while shouting an inspirational message in support of her chosen sports team.

But guess what? When participants imagined what it must be like to be a cheerleader, their test scores plummeted. The stereotype of a cheerleader is that they're sporty and fun but not terribly bright.[49]

The conclusions of the study present us with a helpful technique, then. Bringing to mind a hotshot of a professor can help us to sharpen our wits and perform at our best.

Does this mean that we can actually adopt the traits of other people whom we admire too – people other than the stereotype of a socially awkward but intellectually gifted professor? Actually, no. As we shall see in the next section, it turns out that we can best help ourselves by avoiding admiration for anybody at all. Confused? Read on and I'll explain.

WANTING WHAT OTHERS HAVE

From a professional point of view, I have huge respect for the business mogul and serial entrepreneur Lord Alan Sugar. I had the pleasure of hearing him speak at a conference at which I was also speaking. At the time I was slightly annoyed: I gave a talk that the audience seemed to enjoy, but 15 minutes later when he strode onto the stage, I instantly realised that everyone in the audience would be going home to tell family and friends about how marvellous Lord Sugar was, not some guy called Rob Yeung! Anyway, he came across as down-to-earth and affable yet forthright and determined.

I subsequently picked up his autobiography, *What You See Is What You Get*, and learned that the spirit of enterprise was within him from a young age. He started earning from odd jobs at the age of 11 and was already giving his parents money to go towards household bills before he left school at 16. He set up his first proper business while still a teenager, and by the age of 21 was earning enough that he was able to hire his own father as one of his employees. What comes across from the book is his entrepreneurial zeal – his talent for spotting opportunities and turning them into cash. He's clearly a rampantly successful individual and someone for whom until recently I had tremendous admiration.

I say that I *had* – past tense – tremendous admiration for him because I've now changed my mind. Since reading a research paper that was published in 2011, it seems that admiration isn't necessarily the best attitude to adopt towards superstars.

Let's start by considering what admiration is exactly. I think we can agree that it's a positive feeling of wonder or approval for either the achievements or character of another person. So we can admire what individuals have accomplished or simply the way that they are – kind, funny, tenacious, confident or whatever else. It's a positive feeling because we feel pleased about either what they've done or who they are.

There are other ways in which we can view role models, though. For example, we could look at their achievements and want them for ourselves. We could envy them.

I think of envy as wanting another person's life, their achievements or possessions; it's often accompanied by the desire to level the difference with this superior individual. We can want to level the difference between ourselves and someone else in one of two ways: either by working harder to achieve what they've got or by hoping that they fail and bringing them down. The former type of envy is benign in its intentions towards them, while the latter is malicious.

But does the precise difference between admiration and the two forms of envy really matter? Surely it's merely a technical difference of interest only to linguistics experts and no one else, right?

Not necessarily, according to a clever study conducted in the Netherlands. Heading a team of researchers was a pioneering social psychologist by the name of Niels van de Ven at Tilburg University.

The research crew invited nearly 100 students to read a story about a fellow student called Hans de Groot. Hans was described as an excellent student who had just won a prize in a prestigious student competition. The story explained that he was invited to enter the competition because he had demonstrated excellent grades as well as a broad range of extracurricular activities. And he won the prize because of his 'remarkable intellectual abilities shown during the completion of a variety of tasks'. In other words, Hans was something of a superstar student.

Without the students' knowledge, they were randomly assigned to one of three conditions. In the first condition, participants in the experiment were invited to imagine that:

> *Hans is a fellow student, and you feel strong benign envy towards him. Please take some time to describe how you would feel, how you would react, what you would do, etc., if you were to meet him.*

In the second condition, the phrase 'benign envy' was replaced by the words 'malicious envy'. And in a third condition, 'benign envy' was replaced by the single word 'admiration'. The students were then given a couple of minutes to write down their thoughts, feelings and possible actions if they were to meet Hans in real life.

Finally, the participants in all three conditions were asked to take a test consisting of 18 questions measuring intelligence and creative thinking. For example, one of the questions asks participants to think of a word that relates to the words 'coffee', 'cake' and 'butter' – I've popped the answer in the notes at the end of this book.[50]

Which condition do you think produced the best performers on the test?

We're generally told that it's good to admire people and perhaps less desirable to envy them. But the results showed that, in terms of intellectual and creative performance, admiration may not always pay off. Participants in the benign envy condition on average scored 11.4 out of 18 on the test. Participants in the admiration condition scored only 9.8. Participants who were told to think about their fellow student Hans de Groot with a mindset of malicious envy scored only 8.5.

Before I explain the results a little further, I should mention that the research team also asked a fourth group to participate in a control condition: to read a similar passage about a significantly less stellar Hans de Groot. This time, Hans was depicted as a strictly average student. He had average grades and no more than the usual number of extracurricular activities. He was entered into the competition and got only middling results – he was neither exceptionally good nor abysmally bad. When this fourth group of students completed the same test of intelligence and conceptual thinking, they scored 8.8.[51]

So what does it all mean? The fourth, control condition gives us a baseline performance: it tells us how participants scored when they had not had any exposure to an exemplary role model. This group had only read about a so-so Hans de Groot.

The group who read about a superstar Hans but were instructed to think about him with malicious intent – to formulate cruel intentions towards him – scored marginally worse. In other words, reading about a strong role model does not benefit us at all if we should wish to cause them mischief or harm.

The participants who were told to admire Hans performed slightly better than those in the control condition. But it was the participants who adopted a mindset of benign envy that performed the best on the test: they seemed the most motivated to do well. They worked harder and actually got the highest scores.

'When we compare ourselves to strong, accomplished individuals, it's good to want what they have'

In conclusion, when we compare ourselves to strong, accomplished individuals, it's good to want what they have; it can be beneficial to want to adopt their positive traits and characteristics too. But we should do so in a positive fashion, by wanting to improve ourselves rather than hoping that they will fail and come down to our level.

Why might envy be better for us than admiration? Over 150 years ago, the nineteenth-century Danish philosopher Søren Kierkegaard argued that 'Admiration is happy self-surrender; envy is unhappy self-assertion'. And it looks like he was right. Admiring someone may create within us a happy feeling that encourages us to relax or – as Kierkegaard puts it – to self-surrender. By thinking in glowing terms about someone else's achievements, we may feel just a tiny bit of their sense of achievement, leading us to put less effort into our own attempts to improve ourselves.

Feeling benign envy, on the other hand, may stir within us feelings that we want to be like them. We know that we haven't got what they've got but it reminds us that we want it. And that may inspire us to assert ourselves, to take action.

But how can we ensure that we regard other people with an envy that's benevolent rather than spiteful? Niels van de Ven – the researcher who put together this complicated but illuminating study – makes the point that we're most likely to experience benign envy towards people who have *worked for their achievements* rather than people who have attained their success undeservedly. For example, we're more likely to feel positive feelings towards someone who came from humble beginnings and worked hard to build up an empire than someone who was simply born into a rich family. We can more easily look kindly upon someone who has overcome physical illness, a disability or disfigurement to achieve something in life than we can empathise with someone who was born with stunning good looks and every advantage in the world.

So who do you regard highly?

OVER TO YOU

You may not be the kind of person who looks up to role models, but the research suggests that having a few at the ready could be helpful in all sorts of circumstances.

If you're trying to lose weight, for example, you might look up to a friend, a passing acquaintance or even someone you've read about in a magazine or seen on TV who succeeded in slimming down and shaping up through willpower. If you want to alter your outlook on life – perhaps to become more socially confident or to pacify a fiery temper – you may have other role models who worked and struggled on their issues but ultimately attained the confidence or calmness you desire. Or, as in one of the studies we covered earlier, you may want to unleash your inner genius in preparation for a test, exam or even a business meeting in which you want to come across as smart and capable.

When you want to adopt the traits of a person you admire, begin by finding some way to remind yourself about the person. That may be by cutting out an article about your role model, carrying a book about the individual with you or even downloading a podcast of them being interviewed.

When you want a boost, take a few minutes to read the article, listen to the recording or otherwise summon them to mind: simply sit and think about what you know of them. And then use the following instructions to put yourself into their shoes:

Take the perspective of your role model. Imagine what it would be like to be this person. Try to imagine what you would feel and think if you were that person. In your mind's eye, visualise clearly and vividly how it would feel to be that person.

The research suggests that the effect is fairly short-lived. So the technique is best suited to situations in which we want a fast-acting but only temporary boost. For example, you may be about to go to a party, head into an interview, or have a difficult conversation with a colleague or loved one.

You can wish to have more than one role model too. You might use one role model, for example, when you need to feel more assertive at work, but a different one when you want to feel kinder and more compassionate in your home life. So who are you going to use?

Even though most of us aren't lucky enough to count famed entrepreneurs, sportspeople, entertainers or celebrities amongst our friends, we may still be able to draw upon their support. For example, a friend whom I'll call Marta is an ice figure skater who is hoping to enter and win the British Adult Championships next year. With almost robot-like discipline, she skates four or five days a week and is tutored by some of the top coaches in the country. She spends hours performing drills and exercises as well as running through her routine dozens and dozens of times every week. Her eventual goal is to escape her currently humdrum day job and become an ice figure skating coach herself. But in the meantime, she wants to win the British figure skating title.

So how does Marta prepare? What goes through her mind in the moments before she goes on the ice to perform her routine in front of the judges?

She imagines that she is Yu-Na Kim, the slender Olympic gold medal-winning ice skater from South Korea. Marta sits quietly with a set of headphones on. She doesn't actually listen to music – the headphones are to stop people from talking to her. Then she closes her eyes and imagines how graceful and poised yet athletic and powerful it must feel to be Yu-Na Kim.

Proven by research, the technique works for Marta. Might it work for you too?

ONWARDS AND UPWARDS

➡ In making change stick in your life, remember that you don't have to be the stalwart hero or heroine who forges on alone in the face of adversity. Friends and family can be huge sources of support – providing us with both practical and emotional support.

➡ Bear in mind that both behaviours and states of mind seem to be contagious. Everything from weight loss and entrepreneurship to smoking and happiness can be passed on from one person to the next. So seek to spend more time with people who have already achieved what you want in life.

➡ Give your friends and family permission to remind you about the changes you'd like to make in your life. For maximum benefit, get them to ask you questions about your future behaviour rather than checking how you've been doing so far.

➡ If you're the kind of person who reads biographies or watches (or listens to) interviews with inspirational individuals, remember that you can adopt some of their characteristics at least temporarily by imagining how it might feel to be them. Aim to feel *benign envy* for them; so choose people who have attained their accomplishments through hard work rather than through circumstances of birth or mere luck.

SEVEN

RACING TOWARDS THE FINISH LINE

'Few things are impossible to diligence
and skill. Great works are performed
not by strength, but perseverance.'

Samuel Johnson

When I was a teenager, I couldn't wait to learn to drive a car. Finally, freedom! I had images in my mind of being able to go wherever I wanted, whenever I wanted and with whomever I wanted. No more hanging around waiting for a bus or hoping my parents might give me a lift.

I was so excited when my first driving lesson came around, but in my very first lesson, my instructor only allowed me to drive around the block. My parents lived in a fairly quiet suburb so there was hardly any traffic on the streets. All I had to do was steer the car and avoid hitting any of the stationary cars parked at the kerb – and even then the instructor put his hand on the steering wheel a couple of times to nudge the car in one direction or the other.

Within a couple of lessons, I'd learned to change gears and drive on busier streets. But there was so much to think about! Looking at the side and rear-view mirrors to see what was going on behind me. Checking that my speed wasn't creeping up over the limit. Looking at road signs and road markings to see where I was allowed to drive and whether I should give way to other cars first. And having to coordinate both hands and feet to change gears all of the time.

Each driving lesson took my full concentration. Fortunately my instructor wasn't a chatty man, as I wouldn't have been able to engage in much by way of conversation if he had wanted to talk. But as the weeks went by, it got easier. Within months, I was competent enough to pass my driving test. And now I can drive the car for hundreds of miles and hold a conversation with passengers without even thinking about what my hands and feet are doing.

The first time we try out any new skill – put together a sentence in a foreign language, operate an unfamiliar computer system, cook a meal from fresh ingredients, swing a golf club – it feels clumsy and difficult. We need to focus all of our attention on the task and we may make mistakes.

But the second time we use the same skill, it gets a little bit easier. It may not *feel* much easier – the improvement can be so slight that we may not notice it necessarily. But each time we tackle a task, we become more comfortable with it.

'You won't be able to pinpoint an exact day when it happened, but you'll shake your head in wonderment at how far you've come'

The same is true for when we try to modify something in our lives. It starts off feeling tough but gets easier the more we stick with it.

Decide to go to the gym and that first visit may feel daunting or even downright scary. Worse, the next day you may wake up feeling achy and tired. But keep at it for a handful of months or even weeks and it may soon become so prominent a part of your life that you'll wonder how you ever managed without it.

Or suppose you want to boost your social confidence. You may obsess about the prospect of going to a party for days beforehand. What are you going to say? How will people treat you? And when you get to the party, it may feel pretty nerve-racking too. But getting through one party will almost certainly make the next one that little bit easier and the one after that easier still. Eventually you may realise that you're considerably more self-assured than you used to be. You won't be able to pinpoint an exact day when it happened, but you'll shake your head in wonderment at how far you've come.

The point is that change takes time.

How much time exactly?

A band of health psychologists at University College London is at the forefront in the quest to understand how we can encourage people to live healthier lives. In one particular study, Phillippa Lally and her colleagues monitored several dozen volunteers for some months as they attempted to incorporate small changes into their lives. Each participant in the study was asked to choose a single behaviour that they wanted to adopt. For example, one person wanted to boost his fruit intake by eating a piece of fruit with lunch each day. Another aimed to do 50 sit-ups daily. A third planned to exercise for 15 minutes every evening before having dinner.

Every day, the participants were encouraged to visit a website specially fashioned by the researchers. The participants not only logged whether they had completed the chosen behaviour; they also rated the degree to which the behaviour felt habitual and automatic, a part of their routine that they would find hard *not* to do. For example, most of us find that brushing our teeth is something we do a couple of times a day without giving it any thought. We just *do* it. And most of us have been doing it for so long that it would feel weird not to. So the investigators were interested in how long it took people to feel the same way about new behaviours that they were trying to integrate into their lives.

The psychologists from University College London found that, on average, it took the participants a tad over two months – 66 days to be precise – to feel that they had turned a new behaviour into a habit, a totally effortless part of their routines. But there was a big spread amongst the participants. Some said that it took them as little as 18 days to incorporate the new behaviour into their lives. Others took much, much longer. The study finished after 84 days and some participants still weren't there yet. But by using clever statistical techniques, the researchers estimated that some of the participants would have needed as long as 254 days to turn a new behaviour into a habit.[52]

I mention the study because I'd hate for you to give up too early. In particular, I've read in quite a few self-improvement books that it only takes 28 days – a mere four weeks – to make change happen. I wish I could name and shame the well-intentioned but misguided self-help gurus who write some of these books, but I'm afraid my editor and the legal team won't let me! These authors claim that whether you want to eat more healthily, get up an hour earlier every morning, calm an unruly temper or anything else, it should only take 28 days to achieve your goals.

But that's patently rubbish. We all learn and change at different rates. When I was growing up, for example, I remember a school friend of mine who taught himself four or five different languages including Spanish, Latin and Russian *in his spare time* while I struggled to learn just the one.

We would expect larger modifications to take longer than smaller ones too. Aiming to spend an hour a day at the gym or learning to overcome perpetually gloomy thoughts are plainly going to be more challenging than tiny tweaks such as deciding to write an occasional online blog or wanting to add less table salt to our food.

'There's a huge variety in how long it takes before we adapt to new ways of behaving. The important thing is to keep going'

So please don't hit the 28-day mark and feel disappointed when things don't suddenly get easier overnight. Phillippa Lally's research says that there's a huge variety in how long it takes before we adapt to new ways of behaving. The important thing is to keep going.

LEARNING FROM LAPSES AND FLOURISHING IN THE FACE OF FAILURE

My sister-in-law Emily and her husband welcomed their second child, a little baby boy, into their family just over a year ago. At a recent family gathering, a group of uncles and aunts, parents and other relatives all sat round chatting while their infant son Lucas crawled, rolled and occasionally tottered around the room.

Every now and again, Lucas managed to pull himself up from all fours onto two feet. I think it would be charitable to say that he's not mastered walking quite yet. A quivering pace or two always ended with him in a heap on the floor again. Of course, his parents have checked that there are no sharp corners to hurt himself against, so they're more than happy to let him suss out the whole walking thing on his own.

For the time being, then, it's a case of Lucas pushing himself up and falling, taking a step or two and staggering, and doing it over and over and over again. You can see that it'll only be a matter of months – or even mere weeks – before he's striding confidently around the house. But for now it's a lot of getting up, wobbling, taking a shaky step or two and falling down again.

Now clearly you would never say to a baby that he's a failure and that he should give up! Parents never say, 'This walking business is too tough. You've fallen over a bunch of times today so you're never going to master it. You should stick to crawling around on your hands and knees forever instead.'

But that's exactly what some folks tell themselves when they try to change. When things don't quite go right, they give up. They tell themselves that they're failures and stop trying.

Trying to incorporate change into our lives is just like learning any skill. It's unrealistic to expect that we'll get it on the first go – or even on the second, third, fourth or fifth.

Going back to the study by Phillippa Lally and her colleagues at University College London, the researchers looked at the occurrence of lapses and their subsequent effects. Many of the participants forgot to carry out their new behaviours for a day or two. Some were too busy. On occasion, a few were too tired or simply felt too lazy. But the researchers found that missing a day didn't matter. Having the occasional lapse made no difference to people's chances of making a new behaviour a permanent fixture in their lives.

In fact, surveys tell us that most of us *will* lapse at some stage. In one study, for instance, up to a massive 85 per cent of smokers said that they had tried to give up smoking but started up again.[53] Failing isn't the problem; it's giving up trying again that's fatal, because researchers have spotted that each lapse or so-called failure often improves the chances of success the next time around. The important thing is to keep trying.

Take my friend Sheridan, for example. In the 10 or more years that I've known her, she has tried to lose weight perhaps four or five times. She has slimmed down and put weight back on again and again. But each time she does it, she seems to learn a lesson. She tried a low-fat diet initially but felt so hungry that she often found herself rummaging in cupboards late at night to devour unhealthy snacks. She tried a cabbage soup diet too – all the boiled cabbage she could eat, yum yum! She still felt hungry but with the added side effect that she also felt bloated and full of gas.

Now in her early forties, she's on a high-protein and gluten-free programme, which seems to be working for her. This might be the dietary regimen that will help her to keep the weight off or it may not. But her knowledge about food, healthy eating and her body's un-ignorable needs is continuing to grow. Her confidence in her ability to get to a healthy size is soaring and it's only a matter of time before she will succeed in hitting her target weight and staying there.

There's a somewhat cheesy saying that 'failure is feedback'. But it's true. When we stumble in our quests to achieve change, we may learn valuable lessons that can prevent it from happening again.

ACCEPTING OUR OWN HUMANITY

How do you feel when you make a mistake, suffer a lapse (or relapse) or experience failure? To get an in-depth understanding of exactly what goes through your mind, take a few moments to complete the following questionnaire.

Read each statement and then decide the extent to which you act in the manner described. So, for example, if you almost always act that way, you would put a tick in the box marked '5 – Almost always'. Or if you're not sure that a statement describes you one way or the other, then a '3' might be more appropriate.

	1 Almost never	2 Occas-ionally	3 About half of the time	4 Fairly often	5 Almost always
1. I try to be understanding and patient towards those aspects of my personality I don't like.					
2. I'm tolerant of my own flaws and inadequacies.					

	1	2	3	4	5
3. When times are really difficult, I tend to be tough on myself.					
4. I'm disapproving and judgemental about my own flaws and inadequacies.					
5. When I feel inadequate in some way, I try to remind myself that feelings of inadequacy are shared by most people.					
6. When things are going badly for me, I see the difficulties as part of life that everyone goes through.					
7. When I fail at something that's important to me, I tend to feel alone in my failure.					
8. When I'm feeling down, I tend to feel like most other people are probably happier than I am.					
9. When I'm feeling down, I tend to obsess and fixate on everything that's wrong.					
10. When something painful happens, I tend to blow the incident out of proportion.					
11. When something painful happens, I try to take a balanced view of the situation.					
12. When I fail at something important to me, I try to keep things in perspective.					

To calculate your total score for this questionnaire, begin by adding up the scores you gave yourself for statements 3 to 10. That should give you a score of between 8 and 40.

Next, reverse the scores for statements 1, 2, 11 and 12. You can do this by subtracting your scores from the number 6. For example, if you ticked the box for '1 – Almost never' for one of these statements, then your score would be 6 minus 1, which would give you a score of 5. Or if you ticked the box '4' for a statement, then 6 minus 4 gives you a score of 2 for that item.

Once you've added your scores for statements 1, 2, 11 and 12 to the scores you got for statements 3 to 10, you should have an overall score of between 12 and 60.

The scale was conceived by Kristin Neff, a disconcertingly glamorous educational psychologist at the University of Texas in Austin.[54] What you've completed is an abbreviated version of the full questionnaire, but it will still serve our purposes.

The scale measures the extent to which you have self-compassion – the degree to which you treat yourself with feelings of caring and kindness (rather than self-criticism or loathing) for your own inadequacies and failures. In contrast to every other questionnaire in this book, this time it's a *low* score that indicates higher levels of self-compassion. So people who score between 12 and 28 are strongly able to see their own problems, weaknesses and lapses as part of being human. People who score at the upper end of the scale between 44 and 60 are much more likely to view their mistakes and shortcomings with harshness and even self-hatred.

So why does self-compassion matter? The short answer: developing an attitude of self-compassion will allow you to achieve your goals and be happier too.

The field of self-compassion has received considerable interest in the last decade. Since Kristin Neff published her 2003 paper containing her measure of self-compassion, many scientists have gone on to show that higher levels of self-compassion are associated with better mental health. People who cultivate an attitude of self-compassion – who accept that they will make mistakes and fall short occasionally because they're only human – tend to experience greater life satisfaction.[55] They are less depressed and less anxious too.[56]

Self-compassion can be a somewhat abstract concept to grasp, but I like to conceive of it as saying to ourselves, 'Yes, I make mistakes. No, I'm not perfect. But I'm only human and I'm trying my best.

'Everyone blunders or fails occasionally – and there's little benefit to replaying and obsessing over what's already happened'

There's no point beating myself up for something that's already happened. The most productive thing I can do is to focus on what to do next, not dwell on stuff I can't change.'

An attitude of self-compassion is about accepting that we're humans rather than perfect, infallible robots. Everyone blunders or fails occasionally – and there's little benefit to replaying and obsessing over what's already happened.

To get a keener understanding of self-compassion, look back at the individual statements that make up the questionnaire.

Hopefully you'll see that having self-compassion allows us to get on with life. When things go wrong, treating ourselves with self-compassion allows us to analyse what happened and figure out what to do next without scolding and criticising ourselves overly for it. We can take action that helps us to achieve our goals, to make change in our lives, rather than getting mired in how badly we feel over a single incident or mishap.

The score you got on the questionnaire measured your current levels of self-compassion. But studies show that we can help ourselves to become more compassionate – or at least to deal with individual accidents and misfortunes with greater self-compassion.

In one particularly noteworthy experiment, a team of psychologists led by Mark Leary at Duke University in North Carolina deliberately encouraged volunteers to feel bad about themselves – all in the interests of research, of course. The participants were directed to 'think about a negative event that you experienced in high school or college that made you feel badly about yourself – something that involved failure, humiliation, or rejection'. The participants were asked to write about the event, providing details of the circumstances leading up to the event, the people who were present, the events that unfolded, and how they felt and behaved at the time.

If you think about your school or college days, these are the years during which we're growing up, dealing with our adolescent bodies and learning to deal with all the trials of being an adult – from asking people out to getting our first jobs. So there's plenty of scope there to dredge up recollections that involve embarrassment and failure.

Next, the researchers divided the participants into four randomly chosen groups. The first, control group immediately completed a selection of psychological tests to measure how they felt. As you might guess, spending several minutes reliving an incident from their past that made them feel humiliated and rejected made these participants feel rather less than cheery about life.

The other three groups were taught different techniques with the intention of making them feel better. One group was invited to explore their deepest emotions and to 'really let go' about how the event made them feel. A second group was instructed to write about their own positive characteristics and then to reinterpret the scenario in a more positive way. The final group was asked to list ways in which other people also experience similar events and told to write a paragraph expressing understanding, kindness and concern to themselves – i.e. to treat themselves with self-compassion.

As I'm sure you'll have guessed by now, the group who spent a few minutes writing a paragraph about how we're all human and experience similar failings and rejections in life reported feeling more positive than any of the other groups. Self-compassion seemed to have attenuated the negative feelings they were experiencing.[57]

OVER TO YOU

Studies suggest that self-compassion is a beneficial state of mind that all of us could do more to cultivate. Forgiving ourselves for past transgressions and our faults may help us to become more effective in the future.[58]

Self-compassion isn't about ignoring our flaws and failures or pretending that they don't exist. No, to do that would make us delusional or blinkered and egotistical. Neither is self-compassion about dwelling on our mistakes and misfortunes to such a degree that we get ourselves overly worked up and emotional. Instead, self-compassion treads the middle ground between the two: it's about accepting that we're human, that everyone makes mistakes, and that we need to keep our flops and fiascos in perspective in order to get on with life.

A good start to fostering a greater sense of self-compassion is to look back at the statements that make up the self-compassion test earlier in this chapter on pages 214–215. Read through the statements occasionally and reflect on how you might adjust your attitudes towards yourself.

What's more, if you ever need an immediate boost to your self-compassion, you can try the exercise that Duke University's Mark Leary and his team used too. Say you're going through something particularly tough, you'll need around five to ten minutes to write down some of your thoughts in response to the following prompts:

Remember that having flaws and experiencing failures is all part of the common human experience. It's not just 'many' or 'most' people who experience mishaps in their lives – everybody stumbles occasionally. We're often simply not aware of the mistakes, failings and dark moments that other people experience. So begin by spending a minute or two listing some ways in which other people also have similar failings or experience similar failures to the things that you're worried about.

Next, imagine what an objective but kind, generous and understanding friend might say about your situation. With greater objectivity comes perspective and so your friend would probably be less emotional and more able to see what's good about you and your situation. To capture this more positive, considerate and supportive friend's point of view, write a paragraph expressing compassion, understanding and concern for yourself.

Change is rarely painless; it can be easy for us to beat ourselves up and worry that we could be doing more or that we should be achieving our results faster. But hang on. If there's one lesson I find myself reiterating the most with clients, it's that most of us could afford to go easier on ourselves. We would do well to treat ourselves with more compassion – to remember that it is all too human of us to stumble, forget and give in to temptation. To have days on which we feel we're going backwards rather than forwards. To stutter in our ambitions and falter or fail at times.

I'm a psychologist, so you, the reader, would probably expect that I practise everything I preach throughout this book. And for the most part I do. But becoming more self-compassionate is something that has probably taken the longest to achieve.

Like many people, I spend quite a lot of my working life sat at a computer. This book you hold right now is just one of quite a few books I've written. I also write articles for newspapers, columns for magazines and reports for clients. And then there are the regular chores such as sorting through and responding to emails and filling in expenses claims. Oh joy. Adding everything together, I probably spend around a dozen to 15 hours a week at my computer – let's say a third of my working week.

Unfortunately, not all of the time I spend at my computer is productive. When my computer has booted up and I first sit down, I usually check out a handful of favourite websites. I check the BBC News website followed by those of the *Guardian* and *Telegraph* newspapers. It's important to know what's going on in the world, right?

My next destination is usually my Facebook page to see what friends and family have been up to. More often than not, I dawdle for a while on Digital Spy, a website covering showbiz, TV and movie news. There I'll spend a few more minutes scanning through commentary and gossip about completely trivial (but entertaining) topics such as Lady Gaga's latest publicity stunt, which films have had good or bad reviews, and which sports stars or entertainers have been caught doing something naughty that they shouldn't have been doing. Oh, and if I'm really in the mood to postpone doing any proper work, I'll stop by at Engadget too, a website covering all manner of technology news and reviews, followed by Comic Book Resources, a news hub and blog about comic books such as *Batman* and *X-Men*.

I can easily squander a half-hour surfing the Internet. On particularly bad days, I can delay for even longer and tell myself that I should back up my computer's hard drive or initiate a comprehensive anti-virus scan – the latter alone can take upwards of an hour! And of course none of it helps me to get any work done. It's pure procrastination: putting off work for no good reason other than not being in quite the right frame of mind to get started.

It's one of my worst habits. Some days I can be sat at my computer for six or seven hours but only get maybe three or four hours of work done. I lose *hours* of productivity every week. If I could work more effectively, I could achieve so much more – or leave work earlier and have extra time to focus on fulfilling leisure activities such as going to the gym or reading edifying books.

I used to beat myself up for it terribly; I used to fret that I was wasting time and not living up to my full potential. But now I'm learning to see my procrastination through the lens of greater self-compassion and to accept that it's the way I work. *Oh well*, I tell myself. It doesn't happen *that* often. And I always get everything done that I should be doing *eventually*. My work just doesn't get done anywhere near as quickly or efficiently as I would *like* it to get done.

That doesn't mean that I should give up fighting to overcome my chronic procrastination entirely. But on the days that I do procrastinate, I try to let them go. Accept that it isn't the most productive day and look towards the next day instead.

We each have our very own failings, foibles and flaws. So what are yours? And will you forgive yourself for them the next time you find you're criticising yourself over them?

CELEBRATING SUCCESS

The road to change is likely to be bumpy. We will occasionally slip up, give in to temptation and have bad days. But the good news is that change is possible given perseverance. All over the world, tens of thousands of people every day *do* manage to lose weight, find new jobs, overcome anxiety or depression, and make new friends. Others start their own businesses, find love, give up smoking or other bad habits, start families and so on. And when we start to experience the results we want, it's important to celebrate and share with the world how we're feeling.

In 2011, scholars from five top universities – including the University of Salzburg in Austria and Stanford University in California – published the results of a complex but important study looking at the value of sharing our positive feelings with the world.

The researchers began by recruiting 125 participants to watch a short, amusing film while measuring their emotional responses. Actually, the researchers used two different techniques to gauge participants' heartfelt reactions – one to assess their internal feelings and another to monitor the outward appearance of their emotions. I'll explain each of these before I move on to the results of the study and why we should take notice.

'The good news is that change is possible given perseverance'

First, the participants' internal emotional states. The participants were told to turn a circular dial – like the volume control on a stereo sound system – to indicate how funny they found the film. When they didn't find a particular moment funny, they had to turn the dial all the way to the left. When they found a scene mind-blowingly hilarious, they were told to turn the dial all the way to the right. And if they found something perhaps mildly or more moderately amusing, they could turn the dial a little one way or the other.

At the same time, a camera was pointed at the participants as they watched the film clip to record their every facial expression. The videos of the participants were then shown to expert coders who rated the extent to which each participant seemed to be demonstrating a positive emotion. The experts played the video recordings back, diligently scoring the amount of amusement that each participant seemed to be displaying from one second to the next on a scale from 0 (for 'no sign of emotion') to 8 ('strong laughter').

Finally, the researchers calculated the correlation or correspondence between the joy they indicated on the dials and their facial expressions. For example, let's say one of the participants named Joe found part of the film clip absolutely hysterical and turned the dial all the way to the right. If the expert coders also rated Joe as demonstrating a high level of amusement at that same moment – perhaps his mouth was wide and his eyes wrinkled with laughter – then he would have been judged to be showing a high degree of emotional association. In other words, his outward demeanour seemed to match the internal emotions that he was experiencing.

However, let's say that a participant named Sheena also found a part of the film hilarious – she turned the dial all the way to the right. But the expert coders watching the video recording of her face rated her as demonstrating little emotion – perhaps no more than a wry smile at the corners of her mouth. If that happened, she would have been judged to be showing a low degree of emotional association. In other words, her manner and behaviour seemed incongruent with the emotions that she felt at the time.

As you can imagine, it took the researchers a long time to work through all of their calculation as they had to rate the frame-by-frame emotional expressions on the faces of each participant. What did they do next?

Nothing. Or at least nothing for six months.

Only then did the researchers summon the participants back to their laboratories to complete a battery of tests to measure their psychological functioning. Analysing the data, the researchers' diligence in coding every second of each participant's video and their patience in waiting a further six months before bringing the participants back was vindicated by their finding. Participants who demonstrated high emotional association in the laboratory reported higher levels of psychological well-being six months later than participants who demonstrated low emotional association. In other words, participants who were happy and showed their emotions in the laboratory ended up being happier and better adjusted than participants who were happy but hid their emotions.[59]

'When we're genuinely enthusiastic or exhilarated, we need to laugh and shout, squeal and jump up and down'

When the researchers published their results, they summed up the implications of their study by choosing an apt and pithy title for their paper: 'Don't Hide Your Happiness!' The lesson: when we're happy, it pays dividends to show it. When we're amused, we need to smile. When we're genuinely enthusiastic or exhilarated, we need to laugh and shout, squeal and jump up and down. Stifling our positive emotions may be as harmful as suppressing our negative emotions (see the section 'Bottling up bad feelings' in Chapter Five: Developing Greater Emotional Resilience).

You may already show your joy, but the fact is that not everyone does. And I mention this research study for those who feel it's inappropriate to be too jubilant. Some people believe that it's better to hide their happiness – sometimes even from family and friends. Maybe they don't think it's cool to appear too cheerful or exuberant; perhaps they feel that it's cleverer to be knowing and ironic.

But the research tells us unreservedly that allowing ourselves to express how upbeat we're feeling isn't optional. It's directly linked to our psychological well-being. Stifle our happy feelings now and we suffer later.

OVER TO YOU

When I talk about celebrating success, I'm not suggesting that we should pretend to be happy when we're not – or that we should make a big fuss out of something that we don't truly feel merits it. No, that's another form of unhealthy emotional dissociation.

It's simply a reminder to let yourself show your exuberance when you feel it. Allow yourself to express outwardly how good you feel, no matter how small or unimpressive you suspect others might view your achievement. Don't worry about what other people may think of you.

When I was at university, I lived in a shared house with a bunch of friends. One of the guys, whom I'll call Dermot, was particularly loud and exuberant. When he received good exam grades or was excited about getting tickets to see his favourite band, for example, he often whooped, cheered or clapped. The rest of us in the house poked fun at him and laughed at his unabashed enthusiasm. But it seems as if Dermot was merely protecting his psychological well-being. He gets to have the last laugh!

ONWARDS AND UPWARDS

➡ Remember that change is something that happens over the course of months rather than mere days. Stick with it.

➡ Never forget that lapses, blunders and failures are all natural – if not essential – parts of incorporating change into our lives. *Most* people get it wrong at least some of the time, but we may learn something new about ourselves and how to succeed each time it happens.

➡ Many people beat themselves up for making mistakes and failing. But try to forgive yourself for your lapses and accept that your flaws are a part of being human. Remember that self-compassion helps us to bounce back from failure more swiftly and may help us to perform better in the future too.

➡ Celebrate your successes and share how you're feeling when you make progress towards your goals. Even if other people may not think our progress particularly interesting or impressive, displaying genuine happiness may be an important part of keeping our spirits and motivation high.

CONCLUSION

ONWARDS, UPWARDS AND OVER TO YOU

'Success is a journey, not a destination.
The doing is often more important
than the outcome.'

Arthur Ashe

A few years ago, I worked with the producers of a television show who were interested in identifying what made people happy. The producers wanted a psychologist to interview men and women from all sorts of backgrounds to reveal the characteristics, behaviours and circumstances that separated truly contented individuals from the many people who range from mildly dissatisfied to downright miserable about their lives. The show regrettably got cut short because executives at the TV channel changed their minds about it, but I did get to meet and talk to some interesting people along the way.

One of the women I interviewed stuck out. Ruth – a sensibly attired 33-year-old with the composed air of someone with a deep inner life – was working as a secretary for two partners at a law firm. Every day at work, she took phone calls, scheduled meetings, booked the occasional train or plane ticket, and typed up lots of documents. It wasn't a terrible existence but neither was it anything remarkable or particularly inspiring.

But Ruth had a plan to change her life: she wanted to retrain as a veterinarian. She knew that there were significant challenges ahead of her. For a start, there aren't that many universities offering degree courses in veterinary science so there are huge numbers of applicants for every place. Assuming that she could get onto a course, the training itself requires five years of full-time study – five years during which she would not only be paying fees for the course but also earning almost nothing, as she would have to give up her job in order to study full time.

Another deterrent was that she hadn't taken all of the required science subjects at school. So she would also have to complete a two-year foundation course in biology and chemistry while working full-time at her secretarial job. On top of that, she would need to take four weeks off over the summer – not to go on holiday, but to work as an unpaid assistant in a veterinary practice. Even if everything went to plan, it would take at least seven years before she could fulfil her ambitions.

But, unlike some people who merely have idle wishes or dreams, Ruth was taking action. She was already halfway through her foundation course when I interviewed her.

After a full day's work at the law firm, she often went home to cook a quick dinner before spending a further two or three hours studying. At the weekends, she usually took one day off, but tried to allocate a full day to completing assignments and studying for exams.

'Working and study consume my life. I have to be so disciplined not to go out with friends or switch on the TV. I'm tired, frustrated, tetchy with the family so much of the time,' she told me.

'At the same time I know it's the right thing to do. I'd hate if I got to the age of 60 and looked back on my life to have those "I wish" or "I should have done differently" regrets. I can't say I'm happy and chirpy from one day to the next, but I do have this deep-down feeling of satisfaction. A knowledge I'm doing something I believe is right for me. When I have a bad day at work, I let myself dream a little and imagine what it'll be like to be working and caring for animals and I feel better. It keeps me going.'

Even though Ruth didn't yet have the life she wanted, she was for the time being content that she was working towards it. She was still years away from achieving the changes she wanted and the years ahead would continue to be challenging, but her goals, her purpose – her desire to revamp her life – buoyed her up from one day to the next.

Research tells us much the same thing. People can feel that they may be stuck in all sorts of unpleasant, difficult or even downright troubling circumstances. But the simple act of taking action every day and working towards valued goals can help us to feel better about ourselves and our lives.[60]

As Arthur Ashe (the Grand Slam-winning tennis player whose quote starts off this chapter) said, change is as much about the journey as the destination. It's not simply achieving a goal that helps us to feel happier and more satisfied with our lives – even the simple knowledge that we are *working towards* our goals can make us feel better too.

You can become what you want starting today. Right now.

GETTING STARTED

When I tell people I write books, lots of people say, 'I wish I could be a writer.' Thing is, they could be writers *immediately*.

Writing isn't only about having a book published or making money out of it. It's about picking up a pen and scribbling words on paper or tapping on a computer keyboard and seeing words appear on screen. Whether it's writing fiction or non-fiction, just spending 10 minutes capturing ideas would get them started on the path to becoming writers.

'With perseverance and a dash of courage, we have the ability to alter just about anything in our lives'

The changes we make from one day to the next may seem trivial or even insignificant. But it's the combination of day after day of effort that adds up.

What's your goal? Suppose you're thinking 'I wish I could be an accomplished chef'. Well, why not borrow cookbooks from the library or look online for a single new recipe to begin with? Even learning one recipe every *other* weekend would give you 26 new recipes in a year, which is already more than most people can cook!

Or say your goal is to lose weight. Go for a brisk stroll and burn a few calories today. If it's raining or snowing outside, there's nothing to stop you from walking up and down your stairs at home a handful of times or dropping to the floor to do a couple of sets of crunches. You could even get your heart racing by jogging on the spot or dancing around your bedroom to your favourite pop song.

Even the tiniest actions can contribute to the changes we want to achieve. With perseverance and a dash of courage, we have the ability to alter just about anything in our lives. We can build our confidence, become healthier, adopt new attitudes towards life, get new jobs or start businesses. We can get out of bad relationships or into new ones. We can overcome anxiety, anger or any other emotion, or work towards becoming happier.

You've read the book. You know what works. Now it's time to put the lessons into practice.

So don't delay. You can do it. Whether you want to change only one aspect of your behaviour or quite a lot about yourself, your circumstances and your entire life, it's time to get started. What can you do *today*?

Dr Rob Yeung
www.robyeung.com
www.twitter.com/robyeung

THE CHANGE MANIFESTO

Change is possible. Hundreds of studies have shown that there are tried-and-tested methods and techniques for helping people to improve themselves and alter their circumstances. Now it's your turn, your chance to put into practice all of the theory that we've covered.

In this part of the book, I'll lead you through a straightforward, step-by-step plan for improving yourself or your situation. You can use The Change Manifesto as a manual for helping others to change too. Think of this as your quick reference guide – a cheat sheet to remind you about how to change. If you want to jump-start your own change effort, I guarantee you'll be flicking back and forth across these pages a lot.

1. DECIDE ON WHAT YOU WANT TO CHANGE FIRST

In Chapter Three: Boosting Our Will to Succeed, I introduced the idea that willpower is a limited resource. If, for example, we use up our willpower fending off the temptation to shout at an annoying colleague, we may have less willpower to motivate ourselves to go to the gym in the evening. Or if we exhaust our willpower trying to be more assertive during the course of the day, we may find ourselves less able to forgo having an unhealthy slice of cake later.

By trying to tackle change in multiple areas of our lives at once – trying to get fitter *and* studying for a qualification, for example – we may risk spreading our willpower too thinly. So in a perfect world, we would only modify one thing in our lives at a time.

Of course, you may have several areas of your life you wish to tackle. If so, try to stagger them if you can. While some people make multiple New Year's resolutions, for example, a smarter way to make the best of your limited willpower would be to schedule them one after another – perhaps to look for a new job for the first few months of the year, *then* start a weight-loss plan once you've found a job, and *then* try to give up biting your nails when you've reached your target weight.

'Try to change only one aspect or area of your life at a time'

In summary, **if you have the choice, try to change only one aspect or area of your life at a time**. Get it done, completed and finished before moving on to the next. That way, you give yourself the best chance of success. (And if you want a refresher on the thinking behind this one-at-a-time rule, see the 'Over to you (part II)' box on page 80 of Chapter Three.)

2. UNDERSTAND YOUR REASONS FOR CHANGE

In Chapter One: Getting Ready for Change, I explained that people are more likely to make change successfully in their lives when they have not just good but *great* reasons for making the change. Best of all, recording your reasons will only take you five minutes.

Get a sheet of paper or open up a new document on your computer. Better still, start a fresh notebook or journal so you can keep all of your change-related notes in one place rather than having lots of individual scraps of paper that may get separated from each other.

Draw a line down the centre of the page and write up the headings as below. But instead of saying 'Benefits of changing', you should replace the word 'changing' with your own goal. So it could be 'Benefits of becoming more confident', 'Benefits of moving out and getting my own home', 'Benefits of losing weight', or whatever else you desire.

Benefits of changing	Drawbacks of staying the same

Then fill out the table with as many reasons as you can. **Summon to mind all the positive reasons, benefits or advantages *for* making the change. And note all of the downsides, problems and disadvantages associated with staying the same**.

Five minutes is plenty – and remember that's been proven to be effective by research (see the study by Barbara Müller in the section 'Giving people a nudge in the right direction' on page 23). This step really shouldn't take long at all.

3. HARNESS YOUR APPROACH OR AVOIDANCE REGULATORY ORIENTATION

Did you complete the questionnaire in the section 'Testing, testing' in Chapter One (on page 31)? If not, you might want to do it now. Understanding your regulatory orientation is a proven way to focus your attention and enhance your chances of achieving your goals.

In the section 'Chasing benefits and evading issues', I explained that some people with a so-called approach regulatory orientation tend to be more motivated to pursue change when they focus on their reasons for changing. However, individuals with an avoidance regulatory orientation may be more motivated to make change happen when they concentrate on the problems and issues they're trying to avoid.

Take a look at the examples of approach-focused versus avoidance-focused goals. You'll see that the differences are quite subtle – almost trivial seeming. But remember: studies show that **matching the phrasing of your goal with your regulatory orientation reaps benefits that are far from trivial.**

Approach-focused goals	Avoidance-focused goals
I want to eat more fruit.	I want to eat fewer pastries.
I shall look for the positives in challenging situations.	I must worry less.

Approach-focused goals	Avoidance-focused goals
I will get more organised.	I will stop being so disorganised.
I will grow a healthy set of nails.	I will stop biting my nails.
I will make an effort to compliment my partner more when it's appropriate to do so.	I will criticise my partner less.

So think about the phrasing of your own goal. What will you try to do – or try to do less of?

(4. PUMP UP YOUR WILLPOWER)

This step is optional (which is why I've put the title of this section in brackets), as you may wish to jump straight into drafting your implementation plan. But to ease yourself into your change plan, you could start by strengthening your willpower.

In the section 'Training our willpower' (on page 82 of Chapter Three), I described several studies by the psychologist Mark Muraven demonstrating that we can enhance our willpower – just as we can train up a muscle. Resisting temptation and keeping our motivation high is one of the major challenges whenever we try to change, so pumping up your willpower can be a helpful precursor to your change effort itself.

'Performing small acts of self-control to do with any aspect of our lives may help to bolster the total amount of willpower we have'

The science shows that performing small acts of self-control to do with any aspect of our lives may help to bolster the total amount of willpower we have. Studies have demonstrated that as little as two weeks of self-restraint training may be enough to bolster your willpower for the bigger alterations you may wish to make.

To hone your skills of self-discipline, you could begin by making small tweaks to your life. These little activities don't have to be related to the bigger changes you wish to make either. The goal is simply to practise exerting some measure of control over yourself.

For instance, you could perform posture exercises when you're waiting in queues at the supermarket or the bus stop: imagine someone has attached a piece of string to the top of your head and is pulling you upright. Or practise clenching your butt cheeks for a Jennifer Lopez-like posterior. For a month, you could give up buying expensive coffees from your favourite cafe or decide to swap your mid-morning muffin for a piece of fruit. Perhaps you could keep a food diary to track what you eat or resolve to spend 10 minutes every morning reading a quality newspaper.

There are a couple of further examples in the 'Over to you' box on page 81 of Chapter Three. But the list is endless; the choice is yours. I'm sure you will be able to come up with far more pertinent and interesting little ways in which you could exercise and hone your willpower. If you want to make the most of this change plan, why not jot down two or three minor activities right now that you could do to start boosting your willpower?

5. DRAW UP YOUR IMPLEMENTATION INTENTION PLAN

Most people have great intentions to change. But, as you know, intentions on their own rarely lead to successful change (see Chapter Two: Setting Effective Goals if you'd like a reminder). In fact, change is most likely to happen when people draw up plans to turn their intentions into reality. I hate to sound bossy, but this isn't optional if you're serious about change.

> 'Change is most likely to happen when people draw up plans to turn their intentions into reality'

For example, say you want to eat less junk food and cook healthier recipes at home. It would be of real help to think about the requisite steps it will take to achieve that goal. So when will you buy the groceries? What will you buy? When will you prepare these healthier meals?

For example, say someone called Juliet made a resolution to eat out less and cook more. Her plan might look as follows:

What will I do exactly and in detail?	When will I do it?
Look online for healthy recipes I'd like to cook in the week. Then make a complete list of ingredients I need to buy. This will include at least two dishes that I can prepare in advance and freeze.	Saturday mornings.
Get a taxi to go to a large supermarket to buy ingredients.	Saturday mornings.
Cook a batch of something. I will call this Meal A.	Sunday evenings.

What will I do exactly and in detail?	When will I do it?
Reheat a portion of Meal A.	Monday evenings.
Reheat a second portion of Meal A.	Tuesday evenings.
Pop to local supermarket to buy fresh vegetables.	Wednesday evenings after work.
Cook a second batch (Meal B) of something that I can freeze.	Wednesday evenings.
Reheat a portion of Meal B.	Thursday evenings.
Reheat a second portion of Meal B.	Friday evenings.

By breaking down your overall goal, you will often find that even the largest and seemingly daunting plans can be achieved one step at a time. The more individual steps or actions you have in your plan, the more likely you will be to follow it through successfully. The research shows that breaking our goals down into just one or two implementation intentions doesn't seem to help much. To give yourself the best chance of success, aim to **break down your overall goal into *at least* five separate implementation intentions.**

I realise that the notion of putting implementation intention plans into action isn't exactly sexy; writing out a step-by-step plan is downright mundane compared to some of the wishful thinking techniques that some self-help gurus espouse. This will take a bit of thought and planning on your part. But it's time well spent that will pay dividends later.

6. PREPARE FOR THE BUMPS ALONG THE WAY

In an ideal world, we would simply follow our implementation intention plans and nothing would get in the way. But things *do* crop up. Work can get too busy. Friends may invite us out for lunch, dinner or some other event. Even bad weather can get in the way.

Of course, we can't plan for every eventuality, but we often know what some of the danger spots may be. In the section 'Overcoming obstacles' (on page 56 of Chapter Two), I introduced the notion of 'coping intentions', i.e. our plans to cover any risky eventualities that might crop up.

It's time to draw up another table. On the left, you're going to list possible events or issues that could derail your plans. On the right, you're going to think of ways of either reducing the risk or at least lessening its impact if something does materialise.

For example, healthy eater Juliet might identify issues and her coping intentions as follows:

Barriers	Tactics/coping intentions
Lunches and/or dinners out with friends.	Order a healthy starter and then order a side portion of vegetables with my main. That should fill me up so I won't want a dessert.
Friday nights out with work.	If we end up going for an Indian meal, I can have tandoori rather than a curry, which isn't drenched in a fatty sauce.
When Sam comes over to watch a DVD during the week.	Suggest that instead of ordering pizzas in, we could buy plain pizzas from the local supermarket and fry onions, mushrooms and peppers to add as a healthier topping.

I hope that the examples will give you the inspiration to create your own lists of implementation intentions and coping intentions. **Remember: the more thought and planning you put in now, the easier you will make it for yourself to succeed down the road**.

7. ANNOUNCE YOUR GOALS TO THE WORLD

When you've created your plans, **tell your friends and family about your goals and share your plans**. Many people find they get more motivated to take action when they share their intentions and goals with friends and family. This doesn't mean that you have to broadcast everything you're trying to achieve to absolutely everyone you know . . . Begin with a couple of close friends or family members – the ones who you know will support you – and tell them what you're trying to do. Once you've told them what you want to do and when you're going to do it, you won't want to let them down.

Research also shows that people who remind themselves of their commitments are more likely to follow through with them. In one experiment, for example, participants who elected to send themselves automated text messages that contained reminders of their implementation intentions (e.g. 'Remember to do 15 mins of star jumps before going to pick up the kids from school today!') actually changed their behaviour more than participants who didn't. Participants who sent themselves 3.6 text messages a week on average ended up exercising 50 per cent more than those who weren't told this nugget of advice.[61]

So **use reminders to jog your memory about your implementation intentions**. You could write notes and leave them taped all over the house. You could do something clever with your phone. Or I registered for a (free) online account on Google Calendar (www.google.com/calendar) and set it up to send me text messages (also free) to remind me of things I want to improve about myself. Do whatever works for you. Just remember to set up your reminders!

8. GET STARTED!

The prevailing school of psychotherapy in the Western world is called cognitive behavioural therapy – it's the dominant talking therapy because there's good science showing that it works better than the rest. As the name suggests, the first part of the therapy involves looking at the cognitions or thoughts that we have. But the other part is about behaviour – about *doing* things and *taking action*. And at some point, you will need to turn your plans into actions.

'It's only activity that gets results'

There's a quote by the Colombian author Gabriel García Márquez that resonates with me: 'He who awaits much can expect little'. And I think it's true. By waiting, we achieve little. All that happens when we wait is that time passes. We don't get stronger, braver, more confident. It's only activity that gets results.

The best way to get started is to set yourself a deadline. Decide on a date on which you will take your first step. It doesn't have to be a big step. In fact, a great way to get started is to decide on a first step that won't take much time at all. Make it something that you can do within just 15 minutes to a half-hour.

If you want to eat more healthily, start by eating a banana or apple every day. If you want to exercise more, go for a brisk walk for 15 minutes. If you want to conquer your finances, cut out that store-bought coffee every morning.

If you're hoping to get a new job, you could spend a quarter of an hour revamping your CV. If you're looking to boost your confidence or change your attitude in some way, perhaps call a close friend or two to explain your goals and ask for their support.

And, to make the deadline for starting even more pressing, share your goals with a couple of close, supportive friends. Encourage them to encourage you to get started!

9. SET UP YOUR ENVIRONMENT TO HELP YOU

I've already mentioned that we only possess a finite supply of willpower (and you can re-read the evidence supporting this conclusion in Chapter Three: Boosting Our Will to Succeed). So one of the most helpful things we can do to conserve our reserves of willpower for the stuff that counts is removing temptations from our environments. In our quests to craft the changes we want, we're more likely to succeed by eliminating temptations – completely removing them from our homes, for example – than having to resist them over and over again.

For example, if you're trying to give up processed snacks, cigarettes, carbonated drinks, sleeping pills or anything else, throw them out. Don't keep them around your home or workplace at all. Otherwise, their mere presence will continue to tempt you – and every time you resist temptation you'll reduce the amount of willpower you have for the times you really will need it.

A colleague of mine who feels he wastes too much time surfing the Internet rather than working tells me there's a piece of software you can buy that simply prevents you from going onto the web. When you *can't* do something, you don't have to resist temptation.

'We're more likely to succeed by eliminating temptations than having to resist them over and over again'

I heard a woman on the radio say that she has a credit card for emergency purposes only. To stop herself from going on impulse shopping sprees, she keeps it at the house of a friend who lives on the other side of town.

A friend who decided to read more non-fiction rather than gossipy magazines decided to throw out her rubbishy magazines and cancel her subscriptions. Now, when she travels on the train to work, she makes sure she always has a more edifying book with her to read instead.

What changes could you make to your environment to ensure you stay on course?

10. CHOOSE THE RIGHT COMPANIONS FOR CHANGE

You may remember (from Chapter Six: Tapping into People Power) that social behaviours can be transmitted from one individual to the next, in the same way that the common cold can leap from person to person. **A very positive step we can all take, then, is to choose to spend more time with people who have already achieved what we hope to achieve.**

We may not only learn practical tips from others who've already done it – we may pick up on their positive attitude too. If they've already achieved something, we're more likely to believe that we can do the same.

For instance, if you're trying to boost your mood and feel more confident, you would get the most benefit from hanging around with people who are generally in good spirits rather than those who also struggle with their emotions. Or if you're trying to drink less alcohol or smoke fewer cigarettes, make a conscious effort if you can to socialise with your more abstemious friends. The last thing we need is to be surrounded by people who are all indulging in a habit we're trying to quit.

So who are good examples of having achieved the changes that you would like to make? If you can bring to mind any people – friends or even friends of friends – who have been there, done that and got the T-shirt, you might like to drop them an email or give them a call to meet up sooner rather than later.

Sometimes, we can also help ourselves by reducing the amount of time we spend with certain other people who may not be so good for the changes we're wanting to make in our lives. That doesn't mean we have to be rude to people or reject them cruelly; I have a good friend who is a role model for letting people down gently whenever she doesn't want to do something. She responds to requests and invitations with phrases such as 'I'm sorry but that doesn't work for me' and 'I can't, because I already have a commitment'. Delivering her lines with a warm smile, she finds that people rarely ask for further explanation. Neither do they take offence.

Could there be situations in which you might wish to say 'no' occasionally?

11. ASK FRIENDS AND CONFEDERATES TO KEEP YOU ON TRACK

Many corporations employ a group of non-executive directors to meet together occasionally to give the company advice. They aren't involved in the day-to-day running of the business, but help to check that things are generally going well. In a similar way, I usually recommend that individual clients who wish to get a new job or start a business of their own should also seek the support of a group of advisors. The job-hunter might ask a buddy who works in human resources for help with application forms and interview practice. A would-be entrepreneur might ask friends who work in finance or law for help with the accounting or legal side of things.

> 'The principle of asking for help from friends is relevant no matter what your goals'

But the principle of asking for help from friends is relevant no matter what your goals. If, for instance, you'd like to get fitter, why not ask your regular gym-going friends to take you to their gyms? They can show you how to use the equipment and give you practical pointers on how to get the most from your workouts.

If you're trying to spend your money less frivolously and put more into your savings, ask your thriftier friends for tips on how they make their money go further. Or if you're getting ready to start a family, doesn't it make perfectly good sense to ask friends with young children what steps they took?

Your advisors need not necessarily be your very closest friends. Instead, they should fulfil a couple of criteria:

➡ You should respect them for their knowledge, expertise or skill in the area in which you wish to make change. For example, if you're trying to lose weight, it doesn't matter that a particular friend might be unemployed or have a dismal love life if she successfully lost a lot of weight herself.

➡ You should expect that they will give you constructive, possibly critical feedback to help you stay on course. Sometimes, very close friends who love and support us unconditionally may find it difficult to tell us what we're doing wrong. It can be more helpful to consider other friends who are able to deliver the tough messages that we occasionally may need to hear.

When you've identified the small handful of informal advisors from whom you'd like support, tell them about your situation and your goals and then ask if they'd be willing to help out. In many cases, they will probably be only too delighted to get involved. **Share your commitments with your friend-advisors** and encourage them to ask you how you're getting on. You won't want to let them down and the little bit of pressure that comes from that will encourage you to do your best.

Do you have a friend or partner who shares the same goal as you? If so, you could try working together on some collaborative implementation intentions (see the 'Over to you' box on page 178 of Chapter Six).

Collaborative implementation intentions don't replace your individual ones; these are *additional* opportunities for you to work with a partner or buddy when the two of you might find it convenient to study together, exercise together, cook together, look at online dating profiles together or do whatever else the both of you want to do. The only point about writing these extra, collaborative implementation intentions is to do them *together*.

So who might be able to help with your change project?

12. CELEBRATE YOUR SUCCESS

Whether your goals are large or small, change is possible. The steps we've covered so far will allow you to make progress towards achieving the life you want. When you do start to see results and rightly feel pleased, remember to allow yourself to behave happily – to show your emotions.

Sometimes, perhaps because of the upbringings that we've had, we may feel that it's arrogant or otherwise inappropriate to shout about our successes. But studies show that it's both appropriate and *necessary* to do so (see the section 'Celebrating success' on page 223 of Chapter Seven: Racing Towards the Finish Line).

When you make progress and you feel pleased about it, make sure to show your happiness. This doesn't mean that you have to phone all your friends and brag about your success. But at least allow yourself to experience the emotion fully. Allow yourself to smile or laugh or sing with glee. And hopefully it won't be too long before you make yet more progress and get to experience those positive emotions all over again.

THE MOTIVATION TOOLKIT

As a psychologist, my sole purpose is to help people to change and improve, learn and grow. So I hope that the 12 steps contained within The Change Manifesto will provide a robust, research-based framework upon which you can build your own change effort. Whether you want to make small tweaks to your life or sweeping alterations, you will be giving yourself the best chance of success.

We now come to the final part of the book, The Motivation Toolkit, which contains a selection of mental workouts for boosting your motivation. You don't have to use all of these techniques. Indeed, those lucky readers who possess inherently high levels of motivation and self-discipline may find that they don't need any of them. The 12 steps of The Change Manifesto contain everything you need to make change happen if you manage to put every stage into practice.

However, if you ever feel your motivation flagging or want a bit more confidence before a big event, that's when this box of tricks may be most useful. Say you have a big interview, a business meeting, a hot date or a party to go to. Or you're concerned that you may succumb to temptation and go for the easy option rather than doing the right thing. That's when you may want to delve into the tools here.

In my own coaching work with clients, I find that what works for some may not resonate with others. One individual may relish taking on the perspectives of role models, while another may find positive self-talk more useful. Some find that managing their emotions comes naturally to them while others find it essential to use every technique they can to keep their moods in check.

'We're all different. I can't predict what will work for you'

The point is: we're all different. I can't predict what will work for you. I suggest that you test drive the different techniques at least a couple of times each to see when and where they might be best for you. If you don't like any particular technique, try it for perhaps a different aspect of your change effort. But if it still doesn't seem to work, move on and try something else. That way you will gradually find your way to the ones that are best for you.

MANAGE YOUR EMOTIONS

I'd be lying (and you probably wouldn't believe me anyway) if I said that change was easy. The truth is that most people who set out to bring about meaningful changes in their lives experience difficulties and disappointments along the way. People get rejected, give in to temptation and make mistakes. But the important thing is to keep going and not to let a bad day derail us entirely.

When things don't go right, it's perfectly natural and normal to feel disappointed, upset or frustrated. But we can help ourselves to stay on track by keeping things in perspective and checking that these *healthy* negative emotions don't

turn into *unhealthy* negative emotions. (For a reminder of the distinction, you may wish to go back to the sections 'Understanding the purpose of negative emotions' on page 125 and 'Appreciating our capacity for disappointment, fear, anger and guilt' on page 128 of Chapter Five: Developing Greater Emotional Resilience.)

'When things don't go right, it's perfectly natural and normal to feel disappointed, upset or frustrated'

If we can cultivate our ability to handle the ups and downs of our emotions, we may be able to help the more rational parts of ourselves stay more in control. Here are a few pointers for managing our sometimes unruly emotions a little better:

➡ When you're feeling anxious, heartbroken or otherwise bad, **try the technique of affect labelling**. We can remind ourselves to keep matters in perspective simply by naming the emotion we are feeling and describing the situation. Using our more rational mental processes to think objectively about what is happening to us seems to soothe and calm the emotional parts of our brains. For example, say, 'I am feeling worried because . . .' or 'I am experiencing a feeling of anger because . . .'

➡ You could also **try reappraising the situation you're in**. One way of reappraising a situation is to summon to mind an alternative reason for it. So if you're blaming yourself and worried that things are going wrong, you might tell yourself that it wasn't your fault and that it was only bad luck. Best of all, the research shows that you don't even have to believe the reasons you tell yourself. Just making up different reasons may allow the rational parts of your brain to reassert control.

Both affect labelling and reappraisal are what's known as cognitive techniques. But another way to foil your negative emotions is to get physical. **A proven method for managing your negative emotions is to engage in a spell of physical exercise. Jump around, do push-ups, dance to your favourite song, take a walk around the block, *anything*.** If you can get your heart racing and your blood pumping, as little as 10 to 15 minutes may be enough to elevate your mood again.

SEE YOURSELF TAKING ACTION

There is no substitute for actually getting on with the actions within our implementation intention plans. Start *doing* things and not just thinking about them.

To spur us on, though, we can use the technique of visualisation (which we covered in Chapter Four: Seeing Success). Picturing the actions we intend to take – our individual implementation intentions – increases our chances of actually carrying them out.

'Start *doing* things and not just thinking about them'

However, remember that we shouldn't dwell on the positive outcomes we want to achieve. No, spending too much time daydreaming or fantasising about the results we'd like to achieve may actually rob us of our motivation.

Instead, be certain to **play mental movies that involve the actual steps you plan to take**. For example, if you're looking for a new job, by all means imagine how you would like the interview to go. See in your mind's eye how you will shake an interviewer's hand, how you will sit confidently with your back straight and your chin up. Even hear yourself delivering the answers you've rehearsed for the interview questions that always come up.

Or if you've decided to go to evening classes, say to learn a language, you might picture yourself at your desk doing your homework. Perhaps you could create a mental scene of you sitting alongside your classmates in the lecture room actually wrapping your lips around foreign words and phrases too.

If you'd like a reminder about how to put visualisation into practice, see the 'Over to you' box starting on page 103 of Chapter Four. But to finish this section, here are a handful of further guidelines for effective visualisation based upon a comprehensive review on the topic that was written up in a prestigious research publication, the *Journal of Applied Psychology*:[62]

➡ Bear in mind that the beneficial effects of visualisation don't last forever. The benefits of a session of visualisation reduce by a half after only two weeks and diminish to almost nothing after three weeks. You'll need to keep engaging in regular visualisation sessions to get the most out of it.

➡ Consider that more visualisation doesn't necessarily mean a stronger effect. Up to 20 minutes of mental rehearsal may be useful, but much more time on it produces diminishing returns.

➡ Lastly, remember that visualisation or mental rehearsal is not a replacement for actually *doing* the activity. So running through a presentation in your head may boost your confidence a little, but it's only going to be through giving real presentations in front of live audiences that you will develop your actual presentation skills.

LEARN FROM INSPIRATIONAL ROLE MODELS

This next technique can help us to take on briefly the characteristics of the people we look up to. We may be able to draw strength from someone we see as determined and hard-working; or from someone else who is charismatic and confident. Going to a social event, for instance, we might wish to imagine that we're like someone who is warm and funny.

You may remember from the section 'Wanting what others have' (on page 196 of Chapter Six: Tapping into People Power) that imagining what it would be like to *be* someone we envy means that we can adopt some of their qualities or personal attributes. Many people find this a useful technique when they need to bolster their confidence and motivation in preparing for challenging tasks or situations – such as a high-stakes business meeting or a hot date, a tough workout at the gym or a focused session of study. But if you don't feel that you need to use the technique, then don't!

If you *do* wish to boost your self-belief, you may wish to:

➡ Identify one (or more) role models who inspire you. For this technique to work best, these should be people who have *worked* for their achievements rather than people who have simply been born into privilege.

➡ Find a prompt or cue that will remind you of your role model. For example, cut out a news article about the person, download a podcast of your role model being interviewed or carry a picture or any other reminder of the individual with you.

➡ When you need the psychological lift, use your prompt to bring them firmly to mind and then imagine that you *are* that person. Imagine what you would feel and how you would be thinking if you actually were that person.

For a reminder of how to inhabit the psyche of someone inspirational, you might want to glance back to the 'Over to you' box on page 201. The effect probably doesn't last very long, but it may be long enough to help you at least make a brilliant first impression.

CHEER YOURSELF ON

Another way to get yourself through those tough tasks or difficult situations is to talk to yourself. Again, many people find positive self-talk useful, but that doesn't mean that you *must* use it too. The goal is to feel more motivated and confident, but some people find that they prefer other techniques.

The key with positive self-talk is to repeat a phrase to yourself that reminds you of what you want to achieve. This is *not*

'The key with positive self-talk is to repeat a phrase to yourself that reminds you of what you want to achieve'

the same as muttering broad affirmations to yourself, such as 'I am lovable and can achieve anything' or 'I am confident' when you're actually feeling a bit nervous.

No, cheering yourself on successfully is about reminding yourself of the *specific* behaviours you wish to achieve (see the 'Over to you' box on page 135 of Chapter Five). To inspire your own positive self-talk, consider the following examples:

➡ To appear confident, for instance, someone might repeat, 'I will stand up tall, keep my shoulders back and smile.'

➡ To keep going on a running machine at the gym, another person might say, 'I shall run for another 10 minutes on this treadmill. I can do it. I can do it.'

➡ Someone who's trying to finish a report on a computer might say, 'I *will* finish this report. I *will* get it done.'

You can mutter these phrases in a whisper to yourself or articulate them loudly and proudly (if you don't mind onlookers, of course). You can even simply repeat them to yourself in your head. Whatever you do, stick to specific behaviours and you will help yourself to keep going.

BOOST YOUR WILLPOWER (I)

In the section 'Giving your willpower an instant boost' (on page 86 of Chapter Four), we discussed yet another technique that may be useful for specific challenging situations: writing about our values may boost our sense of determination. It may be of particular assistance when we need to persevere at something that is going to take sustained effort – say when you're sat at your computer with a difficult piece of analysis or a report that you're struggling to write. Or you may want to give yourself a shot of willpower before a sustained session of studying or a workout at the gym.

There's already one version of the technique in the 'Over to you' box on page 103 of Chapter Four. But in case you like the technique and end up using it quite a lot, I'd hate for you to get bored of it. So here's a slight variation of it to try occasionally.

When you need to summon up more willpower, look at the following list of values:

Family	Control	Independence	Integrity
Freedom	Fitness	Achievement	Religion
Helping others	Love	Personal growth	Challenge
Routine	Health	Money	Fun
Recognition	Status	Being needed	Hobbies/pastimes

➡ Looking at these values, start by choosing the three that most resonate with you. You're not allowed to choose more than three – you'll have to prioritise!

➡ Once you've identified your top three, try to pick out the one that feels the most important to you *today*. Bear in mind that our values do alter over time. So try to approach this exercise on *this* occasion without preconceptions, even though you may have completed this (or the other) exercise before.

➡ Once you've identified your most treasured value, look at a watch or clock and time yourself for at least six minutes. Write a handful of bullet points about the importance of your top value. Why is it so important to you? How would you feel if this value were taken away from you?

Once you've spent those half-dozen minutes writing about your cherished value, you will have fortified your willpower. You should be as ready as you'll ever be to take on the challenges in your life.

BOOST YOUR WILLPOWER (II)

Ever since the discovery that willpower is a finite resource which can be honed and developed, you can imagine there's been plenty of research looking at ways of bolstering it. Some of the results that have appeared have occasionally turned out to be rather quirky. For example, University of Maryland psychologist Kurt Gray has theorised that simply feeling virtuous may boost our willpower. But is there proof to back up his claim?

The short answer: yes.

In a clever experiment, he invited volunteers to take part in a test of strength. He began by giving all of his participants a reward of a single dollar straightaway. Immediately, he asked half of them whether they would like to donate the dollar to a charitable cause (UNICEF). Everyone who was given the opportunity to contribute to charity said 'yes'.

When the participants were then tested on their ability to hold a heavy weight, guess what? Yes, those who donated their dollar to charity performed significantly better. In other words, doing good does more than just make us feel better. It gives us a boost to our short-term mental strength too.[63]

So here's a little mental game you can play with yourself the next time you need a boost to your willpower. Suppose you need to have a discussion with a colleague about a difficult topic but want to stay in control of your emotions. Or you've had a tough day but still hope to make it to the gym. To give yourself the best shot of success, drop your spare change into a collecting tin.

BE KIND (TO YOURSELF) BUT KEEP GOING

Several studies have demonstrated the power of self-compassion: **forgiving ourselves for our mistakes, lapses and failures allows us to get back on course more quickly than beating ourselves up about them.** You can remind yourself of the research in Chapter Seven: Racing Towards the Finish Line.

Essentially, this is another technique for managing your emotions. Seeing ourselves through a more self-compassionate lens may be particularly useful when we've succumbed to temptation, blundered in our change project or perhaps suffered rejection or disappointment.

By taking perhaps five to ten minutes to write about something that has gone wrong, you are allowing the more rational part of your mind to reassert itself. I've already provided one version of the exercise in the 'Over to you' box beginning on page 219 of Chapter Seven. But to make sure you don't get stuck in a rut, you could occasionally try this variant:

> Remember that almost no one achieves everything they want on their first attempt. History tells us that there are many famous entrepreneurs, sportspeople, presidents and prime ministers, entertainers and inventors who didn't succeed at first. The pop band The Beatles were rejected by several record labels before being signed and even Lady Gaga got dropped by one record label before her current run of success. The author J. K. Rowling got dozens of rejections before a publisher agreed to publish her Harry Potter series. Many, many other creative, artistic and business people suffered knockbacks before making it big.

> We often forget that other people also make mistakes, get rejected, feel disappointment and experience failure.

'We often forget that other people also make mistakes, get rejected, feel disappointment and experience failure'

> So spend a couple of minutes now writing about ways in which other people also experience problems or failures like the one that is currently troubling you.

> Then bring to mind the name and face of your most sympathetic and compassionate friend. Imagine what he or she might say to you about your situation now. Your friend would never say anything hurtful or critical. Instead, your friend would be supportive and encouraging. So spend some time writing out the kind words this friend might say to you to urge you on.

ACKNOWLEDGEMENTS

First of all, a big thanks to Liz Gough and Jon Butler for letting me try something different with my three books for Pan Macmillan – you understand how strongly I feel that we may serve our readers best by communicating not only what to change or how to behave but also why. I feel that my writing has grown and matured. But I hope I'm not done improving yet!

Thanks to my perennial research assistant Becky Mallery for her diligence and Bonnie Chiang for her remote-control contributions. And thank you to my colleagues at Talentspace for giving me the space to write without being disturbed.

My appreciation goes out to the many clients (and a few friends) who kindly gave me permission to use their stories as examples within this book. I am so grateful. I feel it makes such a difference when readers can see how various exercises and techniques have been incorporated into real people's lives.

NOTES

INTRODUCTION

1 Oettingen, G., & Mayer, D. (2002). 'The Motivating Function of Thinking About the Future: Expectations Versus Fantasies'. *Journal of Personality and Social Psychology*, 83, 1198–1212.

CHAPTER ONE: GETTING READY FOR CHANGE

2 Müller, B. C. N., van Baaren, R. B., Ritter, S. M., Woud, M. L., Bergmann, H., Harakeh, Z., Engels, R. C. M. E., & Dijksterhuis, A. (2009). 'Tell Me Why . . . The Influence of Self-Involvement on Short Term Smoking Behaviour'. *Addictive Behaviors*, 34, 427–431.

3 Higgins, E. T., Friedman, R. S., Harlow, R. E., Chen Idson, L., Ayduk, O. N., & Taylor, A. (2001). 'Achievement Orientations from Subjective Histories of Success: Promotion Pride versus Prevention Pride'. *European Journal of Social Psychology*, 31, 3–23.

4 Tam, L., Bagozzi, R. P., & Spanjol, J. (2010). 'When Planning is Not Enough: The Self-Regulatory Effect of Implementation Intentions on Changing Snacking Habits'. *Health Psychology*, 29, 284–292.

CHAPTER TWO: SETTING EFFECTIVE GOALS

5 World Health Organization (2003). *Obesity and Overweight*. Retrieved 1 September 2011 from: http://www.who.int/hpr/NPH/docs/gs_obesity.pdf

6   Luszczynska, A., Sobczyk, A., & Abraham, C. (2007). 'Planning to Lose Weight: Randomized Controlled Trial of an Implementation Intention Prompt to Enhance Weight Reduction Among Overweight and Obese Women'. *Health Psychology*, 26, 507–512.

7   Wiedemann, A., Lippke, S., & Schwarzer, R. (2012). 'Multiple Plans and Memory Performance: Results of a Randomized Controlled Trial Targeting Fruit and Vegetable Intake'. *Journal of Behavioral Medicine*, 35, 387–392.

8   For just one example of a study showing the power of coping plans in changing behaviour, see: Wiedemann, A. U., Lippke, S., Reuter, T., Ziegelmann, J. P., & Schwarzer, R. (2011). 'How Planning Facilitates Behaviour Change: Additive and Interactive Effects of a Randomized Controlled Trial'. *European Journal of Social Psychology*, 41, 42–51.

9   Morisano, D., Hirsh, J. B., Peterson, J. B., Pihl, R. O., & Shore, B. M. (2010). 'Setting, Elaborating, and Reflecting on Personal Goals Improves Academic Performance'. *Journal of Applied Psychology*, 95, 255–264.

CHAPTER THREE: BOOSTING OUR WILL TO SUCCEED

10 Tangney, J. P., Baumeister, R. F., & Boone, A. L. (2004). 'High Self-Control Predicts Good Adjustment, Less Pathology, Better Grades, and Interpersonal Success'. *Journal of Personality*, 72, 271–324.

11 For an excellent overview of the arguments for the 'hot' versus 'cold' systems, take a look at: Metcalfe, J. & Mischel, W. (1999). 'A Hot/Cool-System Analysis of Delay of Gratification: Dynamics of Willpower'. *Psychological Review*, 106, 3–19.

12 Baumeister, R. F., Bratslavsky, E., Muraven, M., & Tice, D. M. (1998). 'Ego Depletion: Is the Active Self a Limited Resource?' *Journal of Personality and Social Psychology*, 74, 1252–1265.

13 Both of these additional studies – involving the 'white bear' and the upsetting film – are written up in: Muraven, M., Tice, D. M., & Baumeister, R. F. (1998). 'Self-Control as Limited Resource: Regulatory Depletion Patterns'. *Journal of Personality and Social Psychology*, 74, 774–789.

14 Muraven, M., Collins, R. L., Shiffman, S., & Paty, J. A. (2005). 'Daily Fluctuations in Self-Control Demands and Alcohol Intake'. *Psychology of Addictive Behaviors*, 19, 140–147.

15 For a comprehensive review of the many studies that have shown that willpower is a finite resource, see: Hagger, M. S., Wood, C., Stiff, C., & Chatzisarantis, N. (2010). 'Ego Depletion and the Strength Model of Self-Control: A Meta-Analysis'. *Psychological Bulletin*, 136, 495–525.

16 Muraven, M. (2010). Practicing Self-Control Lowers the Risk of Smoking Lapse. *Psychology of Addictive Behaviors*, 24, 446–452.

17 Schmeichel, B. J., & Vohs, K. (2009). 'Self-Affirmation and Self-Control: Affirming Core Values Counteracts Ego Depletion'. *Journal of Personality and Social Psychology*, 96, 770–782.

CHAPTER FOUR: SEEING SUCCESS

18 Oettingen, G., & Wadden, T. A. (1991). 'Expectation, Fantasy, and Weight Loss: Is the Impact of Positive Thinking Always Positive?' *Cognitive Therapy and Research*, 15, 167–175.

19 Kappes, H. B., & Oettingen, G. (2011). 'Positive Fantasies About Idealized Futures Sap Energy'. *Journal of Experimental Social Psychology*, 47, 719–729.

20 http://www.atpworldtour.com/News/DEUCE-Tennis/Djokovic-No1/Djokovic-Tribute.aspx – accessed 16 September 2011.

21 Olsson, C. J., Jonsson, B., & Nyberg, L. (2008). 'Internal Imagery Training in Active High Jumpers'. *Scandinavian Journal of Psychology*, 49, 133–140.

22 Pham, L. B., & Taylor, S. E. (1999). 'From Thought to Action: Effects of Process- Versus Outcome-Based Mental Simulations on Performance'. *Personality and Social Psychology Bulletin*, 25, 250–260.

23 Knäuper, B., McCollam, A., Rosen-Brown, A., Lacaille, J., Kelso, E., & Roseman, M. (2011). 'Fruitful Plans: Adding Targeted Mental Imagery to Implementation Intentions Increases Fruit Consumption'. *Psychology and Health*, 26, 601–617.

24 Several studies have shown that visualisations taken from a third-person perspective (as if you're watching yourself) are more motivating than visualisations taken from the first-person perspective (as if you're seeing the world around you through your own eyes). See, for example: Vasquez, N. A., & Buehler, R. (2007). 'Seeing Future Success: Does Imagery Perspective Influence Achievement Motivation'. *Personality and Social Psychology Bulletin*, 33, 1392–1405. I also discuss this fact further in Chapter Five of one of my other books: Yeung, R. (2010). *I Is for Influence: The New Science of Persuasion*. London: Macmillan.

CHAPTER FIVE: DEVELOPING GREATER EMOTIONAL RESILIENCE

25 Carver, C. S., & Scheier, M. F. (1990). 'Origins and Functions of Positive and Negative Affect: A Control-Process View'. *Psychological Review*, 97, 19–35.

26 The first time I came across the distinction between healthy and unhealthy types of negative emotion was in a book written by Windy Dryden, professor of psychotherapeutic studies at Goldsmith's College, University of London: Dryden, W. (1994). *Ten Steps to Positive Living*. London: Sheldon Press.

27 For an overview of this burgeoning field of study into emotion regulation, see: Gross, J. J. (1998). 'The Emerging Field of Emotion Regulation: An Integrative Review'. *Review of General Psychology*, 2, 271–299.

28 Lieberman, M. D., Inagaki, T. K., Tabibnia, G., & Crockett, M. J. (2011). 'Subjective Responses to Emotional Stimuli During Labeling, Reappraisal, and Distraction'. *Emotion*, 11, 468–480.

29 Hopp, H., Troy, A. S., & Mauss, I. B. (2011). 'The Unconscious Pursuit of Emotion Regulation: Implications for Psychological Health'. *Cognition and Emotion*, 25, 532–545.

30 Gross, J. J., & John, O. P. (2003). 'Individual Differences in Two Emotion Regulation Processes: Implications for Affect, Relationships, and Well-Being'. *Journal of Personality and Social Psychology*, 85, 348–362.

31 Wood, J. V., Perunovic, E., & Lee, J. W. (2009). 'Positive Self-Statements: Power for Some, Peril for Others'. *Psychological Science*, 20, 860–866.

32 Rosenberg, M. (1965). *Society and the Adolescent Self-Image*. Princeton, NJ: Princeton University Press.

33 Bayer, U. C., & Gollwitzer, P. M. (2007). 'Boosting Scholastic Test Scores by Willpower: The Role of Implementation Intentions'. *Self and Identity*, 6, 1–19.

34 On average, people in Europe watch TV for 226 minutes (3 hours and 46 minutes) *every day*, while Americans watch 297 minutes (4 hours and 57 minutes) of TV daily: IP Germany (ed.) (2005). *Television 2005: International Keyfacts*. Cologne, Germany: IP Germany.

35 Blumenthal, J. A., Babyak, M. A., Moore, K. A., Craighead, W. E., Herman, S., Khatri, P., Waugh, R., Napolitano, M. A., Forman, L. M., Appelbaum, M., Doraiswamy, P. M., & Krishnan, K. R. (1999). 'Effects of Exercise Training on Older Patients with Major Depression'. *Archives of Internal Medicine*, 159, 2349–2356.

36 Ströhle, A. (2009). 'Physical Activity, Exercise, Depression and Anxiety Disorders'. *Journal of Neural Transmission*, 116, 777–784.

37 Yeung, R. R., & Hemsley, D. R. (1996). 'Effects of Personality and Acute Exercise on Mood States'. *Personality and Individual Differences*, 20, 545–550.

38 Hansen, C. J., Stevens, L. C., & Coast, J. R. (2001). 'Exercise Duration and Mood State: How Much Is Enough to Feel Better?' *Health Psychology*, 20, 267–275.

39 Yeung, R. R. (1996). 'The Acute Effects of Exercise on Mood State'. *Journal of Psychosomatic Research*, 40, 123–141.

CHAPTER SIX: TAPPING INTO PEOPLE POWER

40 Christakis, N. A., & Fowler, J. H. (2007). 'The Spread of Obesity in a Large Social Network over 32 Years'. *New England Journal of Medicine*, 357, 370–379.

41 Rosenquist, J. N., Murabito, J., Fowler, J. H., & Christakis, N. A. (2010). 'The Spread of Alcohol Consumption Behavior in a Large Social Network'. *Annals of Internal Medicine*, 152, 426–433.

42 Christakis, N. A., & Fowler, J. H. (2008). 'The Collective Dynamics of Smoking in a Large Social Network'. *New England Journal of Medicine*, 358, 2249–2258.

43 Fowler, J. H., & Christakis, N. A. (2008). 'Dynamic Spread of Happiness in a Large Social Network: Longitudinal Analysis over 20 Years in the Framingham Heart Study'. *British Medical Journal*, 337, 2338.

44 Levav, J., & Fitzsimons, G. J. (2006). 'When Questions Change Behavior: The Role of Ease of Representation'. *Psychological Science*, 17, 207–213.

45 Greenwald, A. G., Carnot, C. G., Beach, R., & Young, B. (1987). 'Increasing Voter Behavior by Asking People If They Expect to Vote'. *Journal of Applied Psychology*, 72, 315–318.

46 Morwitz, V. G., & Fitzsimons, G. J. (2004). 'The Mere-measurement Effect: Why Does Measuring Intentions Change Actual Behaviour?' *Journal of Consumer Psychology*, 14, 64–73.

47 Prestwich, A., Conner, M. T., Lawton, R. J., Ward, J. K., Ayres, K., & McEachan, R. R. C. (2012). 'Randomized Controlled Trial of Collaborative Implementation Intentions Targeting Working Adults' Physical Activity'. *Health Psychology*, 31, 486–495.

48 The third rule states that Charlie always chooses to take bus 43, so the correct answer is c).

49 Galinsky, A. D., Wang, C. S., & Ku, G. (2008). 'Perspective-Takers Behave More Stereotypically'. *Journal of Personality and Social Psychology*, 95, 404–419.

50 The word 'cup' would give us 'coffee cup', 'cupcake' and 'buttercup'.

51 van de Ven, N., Zeelenberg, M., & Pieters, R. (2011). 'Why Envy Outperforms Admiration'. *Personality and Social Psychology Bulletin*, 37, 784–795.

CHAPTER SEVEN: RACING TOWARDS THE FINISH LINE

52 Lally, P., Van Jaarsveld, C. H. M., Potts, H. W. W., & Wardle, J. (2010). 'How Are Habits Formed: Modelling Habit Formation in the Real World'. *European Journal of Social Psychology*, 40, 998–1009.

53 Prochaska, J. O., & DiClemente, C. C. (1983). *The Transtheoretical Approach: Crossing Traditional Boundaries of Change*. Homewood, Illinois: Dorsey Press.

54 Neff, K. D. (2003). 'The Development and Validation of a Scale to Measure Self-Compassion'. *Self and Identity*, 2, 223–250.

55 Neely, M. E., Schallert, D. L., Mohammed, S. S., Roberts, R. M., & Chen, Y.-J. (2009). 'Self-Kindness When Facing Stress: The Role of Self-Compassion, Goal Regulation, and Support in College Students' Well-Being'. *Motivation and Emotion*, 33, 88–97.

56 Neff, K. D. (2011). 'Self-Compassion, Self-Esteem, and Well-Being'. *Social and Personality Psychology Compass*, 5, 1–12.

57 Leary, M. R., Tate, E. B., Adams, C. E., Allen, A. B., & Hancock, J. (2007). 'Self-Compassion and Reactions to Unpleasant Self-Relevant Events: The Implications of Treating Oneself Kindly'. *Journal of Personality and Social Psychology*, 92, 887–904.

58 Wohl, M. J. A., Pychyl, T. A., & Bennett, S. H. (2010). 'I Forgive Myself, Now I Can Study: How Self-Forgiveness for Procrastinating Can Reduce Future Procrastination'. *Personality and Individual Differences*, 48, 803–808.

59 Mauss, I. B., Shallcross, A. J., Troy, A. S., John, O. P., Ferrer, E., Wilhelm, F. H., & Gross, J. J. (2011). 'Don't Hide Your Happiness! Positive Emotion Dissociation, Social Connectedness, and Psychological Functioning'. *Journal of Personality and Social Psychology*, 100, 738–748.

CONCLUSION

60 Oishi, S., Diener, E., Suh, E., & Lucas, R. E. (1999). 'Value as a Moderator in Subjective Well-Being'. *Journal of Personality*, 67, 157–184.

THE CHANGE MANIFESTO

61 Prestwich, A., Perugini, M., Hurling, R. (2009). 'Can the Effects of Implementation Intentions on Exercise Be Enhanced Using Text Messages?' *Psychology and Health*, 24, 677–687.

THE MOTIVATION TOOLKIT

62 These final recommendations are taken from a comprehensive review of over 30 studies involving mental rehearsal and visualisation techniques: Driskell, J. E., Copper, C., & Moran, A. (1994). 'Does Mental Practice Enhance Performance?' *Journal of Applied Psychology*, 4, 481–492.

63 Gray, K. (2010). 'Moral Transformation: Good and Evil Turn the Weak into the Mighty'. *Social Psychological and Personality Science*, 1, 253–258.